# Communications
# in Computer and Information Science    **1056**

*Commenced Publication in 2007*
Founding and Former Series Editors:
Phoebe Chen, Alfredo Cuzzocrea, Xiaoyong Du, Orhun Kara, Ting Liu,
Krishna M. Sivalingam, Dominik Ślęzak, Takashi Washio, Xiaokang Yang,
and Junsong Yuan

More information about this series at http://www.springer.com/series/7899

Kerstin Bach · Massimiliano Ruocco (Eds.)

# Nordic Artificial Intelligence Research and Development

Third Symposium of the Norwegian AI Society, NAIS 2019
Trondheim, Norway, May 27–28, 2019
Proceedings

 Springer

*Editors*
Kerstin Bach (iD)
Department of Computer Science
Norwegian University of Science
and Technology
Trondheim, Norway

Massimiliano Ruocco (iD)
Department of Computer Science
Norwegian University of Science
and Technology
Trondheim, Norway

ISSN 1865-0929         ISSN 1865-0937 (electronic)
Communications in Computer and Information Science
ISBN 978-3-030-35663-7         ISBN 978-3-030-35664-4 (eBook)
https://doi.org/10.1007/978-3-030-35664-4

This Springer imprint is published by the registered company Springer Nature Switzerland AG
The registered company address is: Gewerbestrasse 11, 6330 Cham, Switzerland

# Preface

This volume contains the papers presented during the 2019 Symposium of the Norwegian AI Society (NAIS 2019) that was held during May 27–28, 2019, at the Norwegian University of Science and Technology in Trondheim. The NAIS Symposium was held for the third time and the first time since 2010. The symposium aims at bringing together researchers and practitioners in the field of Artificial Intelligence (AI) from Norway and Scandinavia to present on-going work and discuss the future directions of AI. With the symposium, NAIS provides a forum for networking among researchers as well building links with related research fields, practitioners, and businesses.

This year there were 21 submissions. Each submission was reviewed by at least two Program Committee members as well as an additional review by the Program Committee chairs. The committee decided to accept 14 papers presented in 3 technical sessions (9 papers and 5 posters). The program also included four invited talks as well as a panel discussion about the status of AI in Norway.

The symposium started on Monday with a welcome by symposium co-chair, Massimiliano Ruocco, and the head of the computer science department at NTNU, John Krogstie. The first invited talk was given by Agnar Aamodt and Odd Erik Gundersen, on the history and future of the Norwegian AI Society. Agnar Aamodt, who was among the founding members of NAIS in 1985, took a look back on the history of AI research over the past 30+ years, while the current chair of NAIS, Odd Erik Gundersen, spoke about the challenges ahead in research and industry. The invited talk was followed by two technical sessions and another two invited talks. The second invited talk was given by Jon Bratseth on Vespa.ai, an open source platform for storing, selecting, processing, and making model inferences over large data sets at end user request time. Jon presented the motivation to build Vespa.ai, which aims to move the focus from technologies for offline analysis and learning from big data towards making data-driven decisions in real time. The final talk of the day was given by Bernt Viggo Matheussen, from Agder Energi, on "AI in the Renewable Energy Sector." Bernt gave insights in trends and challenges for industrial applications of machine learning in the energy sector and presented current work by Agder Energi on price forecasting, hydropower optimization, and snow estimation. The day closed with a dinner for all participants in the heart of Trondheim's old town, Bakklandet.

On Tuesday, the symposium featured a panel on the current status and future direction of AI in Norway chaired by Kerstin Bach. The four panelists were Ole Jakob Mengshoel (professor at NTNU and director of the Norwegian Open AI Lab), Klas Pettersen (CEO of NORA), Signe Riemer-Sørensen (Research Scientist at Sintef Digital), and Ola Tørudbakken (SVP Rackscale at Graphcore). The core discussion of the panel, as well as with the audience, was centered around the strength of the AI environment in Norway and how the AI community could play an active role. There was an agreement that the Norwegian industry must understand the value and utilize their data by developing AI systems that are safe, explainable, and trustworthy. Moreover, the value creation should take place in Norway, and therefore, we need to invest the AI research – especially in fundamental research. After a lively discussion among the panelists and challenging questions from an engaged audience, the program continued with the third and final technical session and the closing invited talk by Arnoldo Frigessi from the University of Oslo. Arnoldo presented joint work with Qinghua Liu, Marta Crispino, Ida Scheel, Valeria Vitelli, Øystein Sørensen, and Elja Arjas on "Bayesian Preference Learning." He reviewed their work on probabilistic approaches to preference learning, including the Mallows and Bradley-Terry models, and discussed the use of these methods, comparing them to matrix factorization approaches. Throughout both days, we had all the posters presented during the breaks, and participants were discussing them over a cup of coffee.

The success of the symposium would not be possible without the help of many colleagues. We would like to thank the Program Committee for reviewing papers and giving feedback to the authors. Furthermore, we are grateful for the support we received from the Department of Computer Science (IDI) at NTNU and the Norwegian Open AI Lab for hosting the event. The student organization BRAIN assisted during the registration and our colleagues from the NAIS board for suggesting and contacting invited speakers and sponsors. A very special thanks goes to Marianne Lyseng, who kept track of all administrative work and ensured a smooth symposium.

We are thankful for our sponsors who helped to keep the registration fees low, and in particular, supported the next generation of researchers to join the symposium and network with the members of the AI community in Norway. Our sponsors were the IDI at NTNU, Trønderenergi, Telenor Research, DNV GL, as well as the Research Council of Norway. Managing submissions and proceeding through EasyChair made our work a lot easier and we warmly thank EasyChair for this.

Last but not least, we thank all participants of the symposium for presenting their work, engaging in discussions, and actively participating in a lively exchange among researchers in AI.

May 2019                                                       Kerstin Bach
Massimiliano Ruocco

# Organization

## Program Committee

| | |
|---|---|
| Agnar Aamodt | Norwegian University of Science and Technology, Norway |
| Alex Alcocer | Oslo Metropolitan, Norway |
| Erlend Aune | Norwegian University of Science and Technology, Norway |
| Kerstin Bach | Norwegian University of Science and Technology, Norway |
| Baltasar Beferull-Lozano | Universitetet i Agder, Norway |
| Steven Bos | Univesitetet i Sørøst Norge, Norway |
| Humberto Castejon | Telenor Research and Future Studies, Norway |
| Arjun Chandra | Telenor Research, Norway |
| Benjamin Dunn | Norwegian University of Science and Technology, Norway |
| Simen Eide | FINN.no and University of Oslo, Norway |
| Jo Eidsvik | Norwegian University of Science and Technology, Norway |
| Jon Arne Glomsrud | DNV GL, Norway |
| Morten Goodwin | University of Agder, Norway |
| Giuseppe Claudio Guarnera | Norwegian University of Science and Technology, Norway |
| Gudmund Hermansen | University of Oslo, Norway |
| Magdalena Ivanovska | University of Oslo, Norway |
| Aurelie Jallat | Equinor, Norway |
| Trygve Karper | Cognite, Norway |
| Frank Alexander Kraemer | Norwegian University of Science and Technology, Norway |
| Helge Langseth | Norwegian University of Science and Technology, Norway |
| Anastasios Lekkas | Norwegian University of Science and Technology, Norway |
| Gabriele Martinelli | Refinitiv, Oslo, Norway |
| Rudolf Mester | Norwegian University of Science and Technology, Norway |
| Signe Moe | SINTEF, Norway |
| Stefano Nichele | Oslo Metropolitan University, Norway |
| Aria Rahmati | DNB, Norway |
| Kiran Raja | Norwegian University of Science and Technology, Norway |

Heri Ramampiaro                     Norwegian University of Science and Technology,
                                    Norway
Signe Riemer                        SINTEF, Norway
Pierluigi-Salvo Rossi               Kongsberg Digital, Norway
Massimiliano Ruocco                 Telenor, NTNU, Norway
Francesco Scibilia                  Equinor, NTNU, Norway
Lester Solbakken                    Verizon Media Group, Norway
Axel Tidemann                       Telenor Research, Norway
Jim Torresen                        University of Oslo, Norway
Christoph Trattner                  University of Bergen, Norway
Valeria Vitelli                     University of Oslo, Norway
Leendert W. M. Wienhofen            Trondheim Kommune, Norway
Zhirong Yang                        Norwegian University of Science and Technology,
                                    Norway
Anis Yazidi                         Oslo Metropolitan University, Norway

# Contents

**Short Papers**

# Full Papers

# Evolved Art with Transparent, Overlapping, and Geometric Shapes

Joachim Berg, Nils Gustav Andreas Berggren, Sivert Allergodt Borgeteien,
Christian Ruben Alexander Jahren, Arqam Sajid, and Stefano Nichele[✉]

Faculty of Technology, Art, and Design - AI Lab, Oslo Metropolitan University,
Oslo, Norway
stefano.nichele@oslomet.no

**Abstract.** In this work, an evolutionary art project is presented where images are approximated by transparent, overlapping and geometric shapes of different types, e.g., polygons, circles, lines. Genotypes representing features and order of the geometric shapes are evolved with a fitness function that has the corresponding pixels of an input image as a target goal. A genotype-to-phenotype mapping is therefore applied to render images, as the chosen genetic representation is indirect, i.e., genotypes do not include pixels but a combination of shapes with their properties. Different combinations of shapes, quantity of shapes, mutation types and populations are tested. The goal of the work herein is twofold: (1) to approximate images as precisely as possible with evolved indirect encodings, (2) to produce visually appealing results and novel artistic styles.

**Keywords:** Artificial intelligence · Evolutionary art

## 1 Introduction

In nature, all species of all organisms evolve through natural selection by passing their traits to the next generation, but with small variations, to increase the next generation's ability to survive, compete, and reproduce [6]. This is called evolution by natural selection and can be seen as an algorithm to search for an increasingly better or fitter solution. The algorithm adapts to the environment by making small changes, or mutations, to its previous solution, and by repeating this process the algorithm will iteratively find an equal or a better solution. The DNA sequences are passed from a parent to a child, and this compressed representation of DNA sequences is referred to as genotype. A genotype is a complete heritable genetic identity used to pass genetic information from one generation to the next generation. It can be seen as the recipe for the phenotype which is the actual visual representation of the organism. By applying this to evolution, one can say that the organism passes on its genotype with small variations to the next generation. While it is the genotype that is passed through the generations, it is the phenotype that is evaluated and subjected to fitness.

K. Bach and M. Ruocco (Eds.): NAIS 2019, CCIS 1056, pp. 3–15, 2019.
https://doi.org/10.1007/978-3-030-35664-4_1

**Fig. 1.** An example of a rendered image genome evolved with the described algorithm.

The phenotype's ability to compete, survive, and reproduce is determined by its compatibility with the surrounding environment, i.e., a fitness function. If the child of this phenotype has traits that are less compatible with the environment than its parent, the child's ability to compete and survive may not be enough for it to reproduce. The initial phenotype has to produce children with an equal or better genotype to make sure the newer generations can continue to reproduce.

Using this concept of evolutionary algorithm, we develop a program which uses the same logic as in natural selection, to recreate a target image using arbitrary geometrical shapes such as transparent overlapping circles, polygons, and lines. The chosen geometrical shapes can vary in size, colour, transparency, and placement. In each iteration, or generation, of this process, a collection of shapes is created, and their structures are represented as instance objects with changeable parameters. These objects represent the genes in the genotype. We will refer to this collection of genes as an image genome.

To distinguish a bad solution from a fit solution, a fitness function is needed. If the new solution has a better fitness score than the previous one, the new solution will replace the old one and be used for the next generation. Using this technique the program will find an increasingly better solution, and when the fitness score is good enough or a termination criteria is met, the program will stop. An example of rendered image genome is shown in Fig. 1.

Evolutionary art is an active area of research. One of the seminal work in this field is [13] by Karl Sims, where virtual creatures were evolved for the first time. Our work is inspired by [5], where they evolved images with overlapping polygons with genotypes of fixed size, and the resulting images produce fairly sharp edges. In [12] an evolutionary algorithm to reconstruct 3D objects based on images is presented. The work in [4] introduces an user-interactive image evolution system that does not rely on user feedback or supervision. Recent work includes [14] for the coevolution of encodings and representations, [11] which uses stochastic hillclimbing, simulated annealing and the plant propagation algorithm, [1] which uses genetic programming, [3] for evolving fractal art, and [2] for cellular

**Table 1.** Sample gene values

| Type | Width × Height | Colour | Alpha | Coordinates | Vertices/ Radius/ Thickness |
|------|----------------|--------|-------|-------------|-----------------------------|
| Polygon | 200 × 200 | (65, 6, 197) | 0.64 | [[22, 36], [110, 172], [72, 0]] | 3 |
| Circle | 200 × 200 | (243, 159, 253) | 0.77 | (59, 182) | 97 |
| Line | 200 × 200 | (35, 89, 71) | 0.12 | (51, 130), (162, 60) | 6 |

automata-based evolutionary art. Previous work by the authors on evolution of cellular automata structures development and replication include [7–10].

## 2 Methodology

### 2.1 Image Genome Structure

All image genomes are implemented in the program as objects consisting of genes for each shape. Each gene is made up by parameters that define the size of the canvas, the shape's colour, the transparency/alpha of that shape, and its coordinates on the canvas, and depending on the shape, number of vertices, the radius length and the thickness. A shape's initial gene structure is made up by these parameters: The width and height of the target image, an array for the colours with values from 0–255, a transparency/alpha value between 0–1, and the coordinates as x (value from 0 to width of image) and y (value from 0 to height of image). Additional parameters such as the number of vertices, the length of the radius, and the thickness of the line are added to the end of the gene when it is generated. See Table 1 for examples for each of the shapes. Their phenotypes are represented visually in Fig. 2 (left).

### 2.2 Mutation Operations

Any gene in the genome can be mutated based on a set of given parameters in the program. A modification of a specific or random parameter of the gene

**Fig. 2.** Visual representation of the genes in Table 1

is done by retrieving the values of the relevant parameters and modifying them within the limitations given. In our implementation we have included three mutation operations, soft mutation, medium mutation, and a hybrid mutation. The soft mutation updates parameters within a limit, whilst the medium operation replaces existing parameters with new values. The hybrid mutation combines the two former mutations by first doing two soft mutation and then one medium mutation (ratio 2:1). We have also added two mutation factors, probability mutation and chunk mutation. The probability mutation is based on the parameter mutation_probability, set in the program with a value from 0 to 1. This gives all genes in a genome a probability of mutating decided by the parameter's value. When using the chunk mutation, a number of genes in the genome are always mutated. The number is based on the same parameter, mutation_probability, but is multiplied with the number of genes in the genome. Example with the probability mutation: If the parameter is set to 0.5, all genes in the genome will have a 50% probability of mutation. Example with the chunk mutation: If a genome has 100 genes and the variable is set to 0.5, then 50 mutations will take place. This means that there is a probability for the same gene being mutated twice (or more).[1]

## 2.3   From Genotype to Phenotype

To render the genotype's phenotype, a black canvas is created, and then each gene in the genotype is rendered onto the canvas one by one. In our implementation we have used a Python library called OpenCV, as it is capable of rendering shapes with correct alpha values. It also provides simple utility for working with red, green, and blue channels of a 24-bit image. As every gene represents one shape, the circles, polygons, and lines are drawn, filled, and rendered in their respective order, in compliance with the genome structure. The resulting phenotype is evaluated by the fitness function.

## 2.4   Fitness Function

The goal of the fitness function is to measure how close the generated image is to the target image, and to distinguish bad solutions from good ones. Our implementation of the fitness function is done by summarising the pixel by pixel difference of the images and that way determine a score. This score is used to determine whether to replace the parent image genome with the child image genome, or discard it. If the score of the child is lower than the parent image genome, the parent is replaced.

To improve the readability of the fitness score, we convert the absolute score to a relative fitness in percent. The percentage score is calculated by dividing the actual fitness score by the theoretical worst fitness score: The maximum difference (255) in each channel of the image (r, g and b) multiplied by the dimensions

---

[1] The minimum number of genes to be mutated is 1.

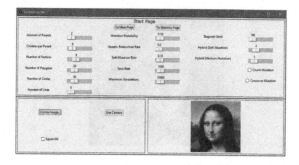

**Fig. 3.** Example of Graphical User Interface (GUI)

of the image in pixels ($255 \times 3 \times$ width $\times$ height). Furthermore, the ratio is converted to a percent and then flipped (100.0% minus the calculated percentage) to reflect approximation towards 100% instead of 0%. The difference decreases as the approximation improves. This way the fitness score is comparable between images of different dimensions and easier to put into context.

The fitness score does not necessarily determine the best rendered image for human eyes. (e.g. image with worse score can be more recognisable than another image with better score.) Certain defined features of an image can be more important for recognition by humans.

The program and data from the experiments are available on GitHub[2].

A graphic interface is available to facilitate the execution of the program, as shown in Fig. 3.

## 3   Experiments and Results

To make the tests comparable, the same target image was used in all experiments. This image was also chosen because it is easily recognisable, see Fig. 4. The initial parameters for the experiments are summarised in Table 2. In particular, the *Number of Parents* parameter reflects how many parents the algorithm has to work with. The best parent has its phenotype shown in the GUI, but every parent's phenotype is saved in the output folder. The *Children per Parent* parameter is the number of children each parent will produce. The minimum value of both is 1, so the program has a population to evolve and compare, and the maximum is set to 100 to limit the processing and the total time it takes. As previously explained, the genome of a genotype consists of a number of genes. The next parameter you see here is *Genes Total*, which is made up of the values of the three parameters below it. The initial number in these tests is 20 genes per genotype. As the experimenting progresses, the number of *Polygons*, *Circles*, and *Lines* will change. The number of *Vertices* for the polygons is an editable

---

[2] https://github.com/joacber/Evolved-art-with-transparent-overlapping-and-geometric-shapes.

**Fig. 4.** Target image used in experiments: Mona Lisa by Leonardo.

parameter, but the radius of the circle and the thickness of the lines are under evolutionary control and are not editable by the user (and therefore not present in the table).

The *Mutation Probability* parameter defines the rate of probability and chunk mutation factors. The *Genetic Restructure Rate* parameter is based on the previous parameter, *Mutation Probability*. If the current number of generations during the process is below one tenth of the maximum number of generations, each gene in the genotype will have 0.1 probability to mutate. The *Soft Mutation Rate* parameter decides the level of change that any gene's parameter can be subjected to. *Hybrid (Medium Mutation)* determines for how many generations in a row the algorithm should run with medium mutation. If it is 0 it only runs soft. *Hybrid (Soft Mutation)* determines how many generations in a row the algorithm should run with soft mutation. If it is 0 and *Hybrid (Medium Mutation)* is not 0 it only runs medium mutation.

The *Save Rate* parameter defines how often the image is saved (e.g. every 1,000th generation). The *Maximum Generations* is set to 10,000. That means reaching generation number 10,000 is a termination condition, and thus the algorithm will terminate. *Chunk Mutation* decides whether to use chunk mutation as a factor in the mutation operations, instead of probability, which is the standard. The parameter is true or false. The functions of these two mutation factors are explained later. *Crossover Mutation* determines if 2 parents should cross-mutate when producing a child. The parameter is true or false. The child is made up of the main parent's coordinates and shape relevant parameters, and the second parent's colour and alpha values.

### 3.1 Number of Vertices

The initial test was to determine the most appropriate number of vertices to use in further testing of polygons. All tests were executed 15 times. Using a genome consisting of 20 polygons, we were able to determine the number of vertices with the most positive impact on the fitness score over 10,000 generations. The best average score was achieved by genomes consisting of polygons with 8 vertices, followed by 10 and 15 (see Table 3). The top graph in Fig. 5 displays the average

**Table 2.** Initial test parameter values

| Parameter name | Parameter value |
| --- | --- |
| Number of Parents | 1 |
| Children per Parent | 1 |
| Genes Total | 20 |
| Polygons | 20 |
| Circles | 0 |
| Lines | 0 |
| Vertices | 3 |
| Mutation Probability | 0.1 |
| Genetic Restructure Rate | 0 |
| Soft Mutation Rate | 0.1 |
| Hybrid (Soft Mutation) | 0 |
| Hybrid (Medium Mutation) | 0 |
| Chunk Mutation | False |
| Crossover Mutation | False |
| Save Rate | 1,000 |
| Maximum Generations | 10,000 |

**Table 3.** Top results from the vertices tests

| Rank | Number of vertices | Average score | Average relative score |
| --- | --- | --- | --- |
| 1 | 8 | 2,885,838 | 90.57% |
| 2 | 10 | 3,014,961 | 90.15% |
| 3 | 15 | 3,032,196 | 90.09% |

results of 15 tests with the number of vertices increasing from 3 to 20. The differences are apparently small. The bottom graph in the same figure displays the standard deviation (STD). If the fitness score has a high variation during the process, the STD value will also be high. Here we can see that the STD value is relatively dynamic in the first 5,000 generations, but flattens out later. This makes sense because in the early stages the image is being created from scratch, and later on the image is mostly being fine-tuned (Examples in Fig. 6).

## 3.2   Polygons

Using genomes consisting only of polygons with 8 vertices, we found that the fitness score increases almost linearly with an increase in the genome complexity (more polygons). The genome size was increased by 5 after 15 consecutive runs with the same parameters. We saw that the bigger leaps in fitness happened between 5 and 15 polygons (see top graph in Fig. 7) - hitting 3,072,442

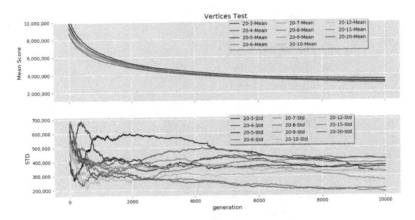

**Fig. 5.** Results from the vertices test with 20 polygons and a number of vertices. Top graph: average result from all the vertices tests. Bottom graph: standard deviation from the same tests.

**Fig. 6.** Samples from the vertices tests (10,000 generations), with 3, 8, and 20 vertices.

(89.96%) average score at 15 contrary to 4,391,165 (85.65%) at 5. 20 polygons is the milestone hitting 2,996,858 (90.21%) average score, and 25 polygons subsequently hitting 2,751,771 (91.01%) average score with an increase of 0.80% points. Increases were minimal with more complex genomes and disproportionate increases in process time up to 40 polygons, with fitness score even dropping between 40 (Avg. Score: 2,494,330) and 50 (Avg. Score: 2,507,859) polygons, thus making 25 polygons the apparent winner for 10,000 generations with an approximation of above 90% and a relatively big increase (0.80% points) from 20 polygons. In the bottom graph of Fig. 7, we can see that the STD value flattens out after 4,000 generations (Examples in Fig. 8).

### 3.3 Circles

Using genomes consisting only of circles, testing showed that, similarly to polygons, the fitness score increases steadily when adding more circles to the genome (see Fig. 9). An all circles genome gets an average approximation of over 90% at 15 circles. (Whereas polygons were right below that at 15.) The increases in

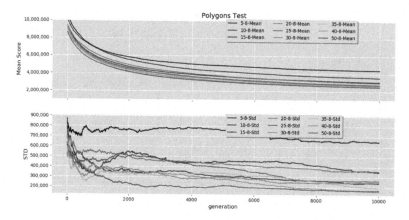

**Fig. 7.** Results from polygons tests with 8 vertices and increasing number of polygons. The legend shows number of polygons - number of vertices

**Fig. 8.** Samples from polygon tests (10,000 generations), with 5, 25, and 50 polygons.

fitness score when increasing genome complexity are more volatile with circles than polygons. We only tested up to 40 circles per genome and do not know if average fitness score decreases between 40 and 50 circles as with polygons. Using 40 circles was however only slightly better than using 35 (92.20% over 92.15% (0.05% point increase)), whereas using 30 circles was a great deal better than using 25 (91.75% over 91.17% (0.58% point increase)). There are no clear winners, but genomes consisting of 15, 20 and 30 circles stand out among the rest (Examples in Fig. 10).

### 3.4 Lines

Testing with genomes consisting only of lines was shown to be an ineffective option. Starting at an average approximation of 65.50% using 5 lines in the genome, ending at an average approximation of 83.86% using 40 lines per genome. While using lines is worse at getting desired fitness results, it may still provide a certain aesthetic and artistic value for human eyes. And may prove useful in approximating certain pictures containing elements with straight lines (Examples in Fig. 11).

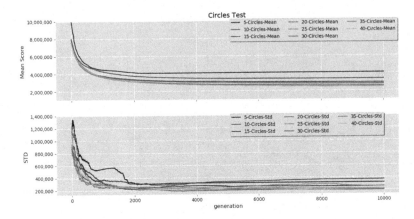

**Fig. 9.** Result from the circles tests from 5 to 40 circles. Top graph: Collection of the circles tests. Bottom graph: The STD flattens out already after 2,000 generations. The legend shows number of circles.

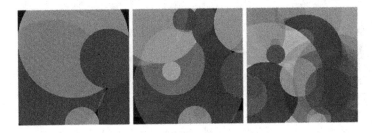

**Fig. 10.** Samples from the circles tests (10,000 generations), with 5, 20, and 40 circles.

## 3.5   Combinations of Polygons, Circles, and Lines

To determine if a combination of different genes had any advantage over single gene types, we tested 6 different compositions with 20 genes in total. The tests showed that the combination of circles and polygons had the best results. The best composition of genes was a 1:1 ratio of polygons and circles, and the second best a 3:1 ratio of polygons to circles. Based on the experiments, lines make very little impact on the fitness results over the course of 10,000 generations, but they may provide functionality for certain images and artistic purposes (Examples in Fig. 12).

## 3.6   Mutation Probability

To find the best mutation probability we chose to only do tests on the smallest population size of 1, due to computational time. The result showed that a mutation probability higher than 50% overall gave poor results over 10,000 generations.

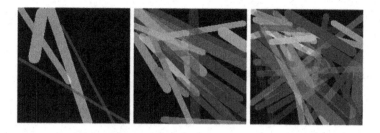

**Fig. 11.** Samples from the lines tests (10,000 generations), with 5, 20 and 40 lines

**Fig. 12.** Samples from the gene combination tests (10,000 generations) with [10 Circles 10 Poly], [5 Circles 15 Polygons], [5 Circles 5 Polygons 10 Lines]

This prompted us to limit the future testing to 10% and 30%. A mutation probability of 10% entails that every single gene has a 10:1 chance of mutating. One genome consisting of 40 genes will *on average* have 4 of its genes mutated every generation. If the probability is 30%, then the average will be 12 genes per generation.

## 4  Other Considerations

After thorough testing, we have found a collection of *suitable values* for every parameter to produce visually pleasing results. Some of the values disproportionately increase the computation time, and are therefore not beneficial even if they produce a better fitness. Some parameter values that have been omitted might have potential to give aesthetically pleasing or interesting results. Interestingly, some of the parameters we tested did not have the impact we initially thought they would, such as *Lines* and *Crossover*, and have been omitted from the collection. Polygons and circles were both relatively good at around 25 genes, and are therefore both represented at 25 in order to maintain a 1:1 ratio, which was the best distribution of genes in the tests.

## 5  Conclusions

Our work shows that it is possible to generate artistic images through evolutionary algorithms, and could be used for artistic purposes. We have certainly been amazed and puzzled by the images our algorithm has produced. Some examples are shown below in the Appendix.

## Appendix

See Figs. 13, 14 and 15.

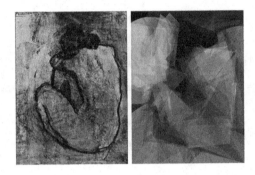

**Fig. 13.** Blue Nude by Pablo Picasso

**Fig. 14.** Google Chrome logo

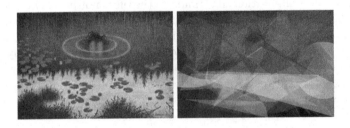

**Fig. 15.** Nokken by Theodor Kittelsen

# References

1. Alsing, R.: Genetic programming: evolution of Mona Lisa (2008)
2. Ashlock, D., Tsang, J.: Evolved art via control of cellular automata. In: 2009 IEEE Congress on Evolutionary Computation, pp. 3338–3344. IEEE (2009)
3. Ashlock, D., Tsang, J.: Evolving fractal art with a directed acyclic graph genetic programming representation. In: 2015 IEEE Congress on Evolutionary Computation (CEC), pp. 2137–2144. IEEE (2015)
4. Bergen, S.R.: Evolving stylized images using a user-interactive genetic algorithm. In: Proceedings of the 11th Annual Conference Companion on Genetic and Evolutionary Computation Conference: Late Breaking Papers, pp. 2745–2752. ACM (2009)
5. Dong, L., Li, C., Chen, X., Tarimo, W.: Evolving images using transparent overlapping polygons (2013). https://github.com/wtarimo/EvolvingImages
6. Dorin, A.: Biological Bits. A Brief Guide to the Ideas and Artefacts of Computational Artificial Life. Animaland, Melbourne (2014)
7. Nichele, S., Glover, T.E., Tufte, G.: Genotype regulation by self-modifying instruction-based development on cellular automata. In: Handl, J., Hart, E., Lewis, P.R., López-Ibáñez, M., Ochoa, G., Paechter, B. (eds.) PPSN 2016. LNCS, vol. 9921, pp. 14–25. Springer, Cham (2016). https://doi.org/10.1007/978-3-319-45823-6_2
8. Nichele, S., Ose, M.B., Risi, S., Tufte, G.: CA-NEAT: evolved compositional pattern producing networks for cellular automata morphogenesis and replication. IEEE Trans. Cogn. Dev. Syst. $10(3)$, 687–700 (2018)
9. Nichele, S., Tufte, G.: Evolutionary growth of genomes for the development and replication of multicellular organisms with indirect encoding. In: 2014 IEEE International Conference on Evolvable Systems, pp. 141–148. IEEE (2014)
10. Nichele, S., Tufte, G.: Morphogenesis and replication of multi-cellular organisms with evolved variable length self-modifying genomes. In: Proceedings of the European Conference on Artificial Life 13, p. 42. MIT Press (2015)
11. Paauw, M., van den Berg, D.: Paintings, polygons and plant propagation. In: Ekárt, A., Liapis, A., Castro Pena, M.L. (eds.) EvoMUSART 2019. LNCS, vol. 11453, pp. 84–97. Springer, Cham (2019). https://doi.org/10.1007/978-3-030-16667-0_6
12. do Rego, R.L.M.E., Bassani, H.F., Araujo, A.F.R., de Lima Neto, F.B.: Evolutionary algorithm for 3D object reconstruction from images. In: 2006 Ninth Brazilian Symposium on Neural Networks (SBRN 2006), pp. 54–59, October 2006. https://doi.org/10.1109/SBRN.2006.17
13. Sims, K.: Artificial evolution for computer graphics. ACM $25(4)$, 319–328 (1991)
14. Sipper, M., Moore, J.H.: OMNIREP: originating meaning by coevolving encodings and representations. Memetic Comput. $11(3)$, 251–261 (2019)

# Activity Recognition and Prediction in Real Homes

Flávia Dias Casagrande[(⊠)] and Evi Zouganeli

OsloMet – Oslo Metropolitan University, Pilestredet 35, 0166 Oslo, Norway
{flacas,evizou}@oslomet.no

**Abstract.** In this paper, we present work in progress on activity recognition and prediction in real homes using either binary sensor data or depth video data. We present our field trial and set-up for collecting and storing the data, our methods, and our current results. We compare the accuracy of predicting the next binary sensor event using probabilistic methods and Long Short-Term Memory (LSTM) networks, include the time information to improve prediction accuracy, as well as predict both the next sensor event and its time of occurrence using one LSTM model. We investigate transfer learning between apartments and show that it is possible to pre-train the model with data from other apartments and achieve good accuracy in a new apartment straight away. In addition, we present preliminary results from activity recognition using low resolution depth video data from seven apartments, and classify four activities – no movement, standing up, sitting down, and TV interaction – by using a relatively simple processing method where we apply an Infinite Impulse Response (IIR) filter to extract movements from the frames prior to feeding them to a convolutional LSTM network for the classification.

**Keywords:** Smart home · Sequence prediction · Time prediction · Binary sensors · Recurrent neural network · Probabilistic methods

## 1 Introduction

The Assisted Living project is an interdisciplinary project with expertise in the fields of smart-home technology, machine learning, nursing and occupational therapy, and ethics. The aim is to develop assisted living technology (ALT) to support older adults with mild cognitive impairment or dementia (MCI/D) live a safe and independent life at home [25]. MCI and dementia involve a cognitive decline that can affect attention, concentration, memory, comprehension, reasoning, and problem solving. A number of research studies have investigated functions in smart-home environments to support older adults in general, and those with MCI/D in particular, in their everyday life. These include assisting functions such as prompting with reminders or encouragement, diagnosis tools,

Financed by the Norwegian Research Council under the SAMANSVAR programme (247620/O70).

K. Bach and M. Ruocco (Eds.): NAIS 2019, CCIS 1056, pp. 16–27, 2019.
https://doi.org/10.1007/978-3-030-35664-4_2

as well as alarm creation, prediction, anticipation, and prevention of hazardous situations. The majority of these functions requires reliable activity/action recognition and prediction algorithms to work properly. This field is at a quite early stage at the moment. With the exception of fall detection, there are currently no commercial systems with such functionality nor are there any complete prototypes available at research and development level.

The aim of our work is to use activity prediction to realize support functions for older adults with MCI/D. In this paper we present work in progress on action/activity recognition and prediction using data from real homes, seven apartments, each with one older adult resident over 65 years old – the majority over 80 years old. We use binary sensors as well as a low resolution depth video camera that is in fact a commercial fall detection system called Room-Mate [1]. We present results on activity prediction based on the binary sensors, where we compare probabilistic methods and neural networks, include the time information and predict the time of occurrence as well as the next sensor event, and investigate transfer learning between apartments. In addition, we present preliminary results from action recognition based on video frames that contain movement information.

## 2 Related Work

### 2.1 Activity Prediction Using Binary Sensors

Several sequential data prediction algorithms have been investigated in the past years [21]. The Active LeZi (ALZ) is a probabilistic method that has been extensively employed for prediction on sequential data [10]. Based on the ALZ, the Sequence Prediction via Enhanced Episode Discovery (SPEED) algorithm was implemented [2]. Recurrent neural network (RNN) models – Echo State Network (ESN), Back Propagation Through Time (BPTT), and Real Time Recurrent Learning (RTRL) – were applied and the ESN performed better when predicting the next sensor in a sequence [13].

Activity prediction includes mainly two tasks: sequence prediction and time prediction. In addition to sequence prediction, the algorithms mentioned above should also be able to predict when the next symbol (representing either a sensor or an activity) will occur. Several algorithms have been used to predict the time of occurrence alone, such as the time series methods Autoregressive Moving Average (ARMA) and Autoregressive Integrated Moving Average (ARIMA) [5]; non-linear Autoregressive Network (NARX), Elman network to predict a sensor activation's start and end time [14]; decision trees [16]; Poisson process [15].

To our knowledge, only one work predicts both sensor event and time in the same model [17]. This work uses a Bayesian network and predicts the next location, time of day (slots of 3 h through the day), and day of the week with reported accuracies of 46–60%, 66–87% and 89–97%. Subsequently, the activity is predicted with an accuracy of 61–64% based on a combination of these features. They use data from testbeds. Our dataset was collected from a real home, it contains events from fifteen binary sensors, i.e. twice as many as used in [13,14], less than one third of the number of sensors used in the Mavlab testbed [2,10, 16], and half of [17]. Our work predicts the next sensor event and the time of occurrence for a set with 15 sensors in the same model using LSTM networks.

## 2.2 Activity Recognition Using Depth Video Data

There is strong evidence that technology can support aging at home [18] and a large number of studies have implemented assistive technology to support older adults live a safe and independent life at home [4]. Human activity recognition (HAR) has been well studied in the past years [24] and a number of algorithms have been used. Hidden Markov Models (HMM) achieved a maximum accuracy of 97% with the MSR Action3D dataset with skeleton data histograms fed to a HMM [22]. Yang et al. [23] reached 97% accuracy on the same dataset by using Depth Motion Maps and Histogram of Oriented Gradients (DMM-HOG) features and SVM. Convolutional neural networks have achieved remarkable results for HAR from depth data. Wang et al. [20] achieved 100% accuracy on the same action dataset with a deep convolutional network by using weighted hierarchical DMMs of the video sequences.

## 3    Field Trial

Our field trial involves seven independent one-bedroom apartments within a community care facility for people over 65 years old. Each apartment comprises a bedroom, a living room, open kitchen area, a bathroom, and an entrance hall (Fig. 1). Our set of sensors contains motion, magnetic, and power sensors. These enable inference of occupancy patterns (movement around the apartment) and some daily and leisure activities. Unfortunately, not all apartments could have the exact same set of sensors due to physical limitations (e.g. fridge door with a too big gap to enable the use of magnetic sensor) and/or different equipment (e.g. residents either have a coffee machine or a kettle). However, all the participants had the same initial proposal of set of sensors, as shown in Fig. 1. There are two RoomMate depth video cameras in each apartment, one in the living room and kitchen area, the other in the bedroom area, as shown in Fig. 1. The RoomMate is an infra-red (IR)-based depth sensor and measures the distance of surfaces to the camera by time-of-flight (TOF) technology. The resolution is $160 \times 120$ pixels, with a rate of 25 frames per second. This is rather low resolution – a fact that is advantageous with respect to privacy, but makes data processing quite challenging.

## 4    Activity Prediction Using Binary Sensors

### 4.1    Data Preprocessing

The preparation of the binary data includes two steps: data correction and data conversion. The data correction is necessary because the data acquired from

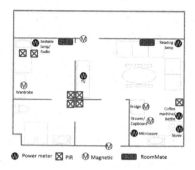

**Fig. 1.** Sensors system installed in the field trial apartment.

**Table 1.** Binary sensors data

| Timestamp | Sensor ID | Sensor message |
|-----------|-----------|----------------|
| 01.09.2017 07:58:40 | 4 | 1 |
| 01.09.2017 07:59:02 | 10 | 1 |
| 01.09.2017 08:03:05 | 10 | 0 |

binary sensors often contain faulty events [9]. In our system, occasionally the motion sensors do not send an activation event when they should. Missing sensor events have been inserted to correct for this. For example, it is not possible to go to the bedroom directly from the kitchen without passing through the living room. When the living room activation event is missing, it is inserted. The time of the inserted event is the mean between the previous and next event. This does not compromise the dataset accuracy because the faulty events are usually between relatively fast motions around the apartment, hence the elapsed time is short. Subsequently, the corrected data is converted to sequences of letters. This is inspired by the SPEED algorithm [2]. Upper- and lower- case letters represent a sensor's "on" and "off" events. For the sample data in Table 1, SPEED would generate the sequence "ABb", where sensors 4 and 10 are assigned the letters a/A and b/B, respectively. Afterwards, we include the time information. This is done in two ways as follows. In all cases the generated sensor events are treated as independent events, as presented also in the next section.

**Sensor Event with Elapsed Time Classes.** Here we use two fixed sets of time intervals: [<1 min, 1–15 min, 15 min–1 h, >1 h] and [<1 min, 1–5 min, 5–15 min, 15–30 min, 30 min–1 h, 1–2 h, 2–5 h]. This results in a 4-class case and an 8-class case.

**Sensor and Time-Cluster with Hour of the Day and Elapsed Time to the Next Event.** We apply the K-means algorithm to cluster each sensor event according to the hour of the day occurrence and the time elapsed to the following sensor event. In the K-means algorithm the samples of each sensor are classified into K clusters such that the sum of square distances (SSD) within the clusters is minimized [3]. Each cluster contains a centroid, given by the mean value of each feature of the algorithm. We perform K-means for a maximum number of clusters (K) equal to 8 and choose the best K manually according to the elbow method [12].

### 4.2   Probabilistic Methods

Both ALZ and SPEED translate the data acquired from the sensors into a sequence of letters and identify patterns that occur frequently [7,8]. The patterns and their frequency of occurrence are used to generate a tree, which is then used to calculate the next most probable event to occur based on the Prediction Partial Matching algorithm (PPM) [2].

### 4.3   Long Short-Term Memory Network

RNN has been broadly applied to sequence prediction due to its property of keeping an internal memory. Hence, it attains a good performance for inputs that are sequential in time. The LSTM is an RNN architecture designed to be better at storing and accessing information than the standard RNN [11]. In this work the LSTM network is configured as a text generation network. The number of inputs is a certain number of symbols (sensor events with numbers indicating time) – equal to the memory length – and the output is the predicted next symbol in the sequence (Fig. 2). The input and output are one-hot encoded. Hence, our input vector has as many values as the number of symbols in the sequence. In the case of 15 sensors, we have 30 inputs to represent the "on" and "off" states of each of these. E.g. when the 4-class interval is taken into account, the number of inputs is multiplied by 4 (120 inputs in total) and similarly in the other cases.

A stateless LSTM network model was implemented in Python 3 using Keras open source library for neural networks. The memory length (i.e. number of previous events used to predict the next event) [6] had value 10. The model has one hidden layer with hyperbolic tangent activation and 64 neurons. Our batch size (i.e. number of samples used for training each iteration of the epoch) was 512. We used Adam as the optimization function with learning rate of 0.01 and categorical cross-entropy as loss function. The output layer was a softmax activation function. We used the early stopping method to avoid overfitting and unnecessary computations, allowing a maximum of 200 epochs for each model's training.

### 4.4   Sensor Event Prediction Using Binary Data

In this section we compare four methods, two probabilistic and two neural networks. In all cases, the results show the mean accuracy achieved using a 5-fold cross-validation process (using 60% of the data for training, 20% for validation,

| Data Processing | | | LSTM Network | | | |
|---|---|---|---|---|---|---|
| **sensors** | **representation** | Data sample | Data conversion for elapsed time 3-classes | | | |
| 1 | A (on), a (off) | 01.July.18 14:00:00;  1; 1 | B0, C1, c3, a0 | | | |
| 2 | B (on), b (off) | 01.July.18 14:00:30;  2; 1 | One-hot encode | 0100 | 0010 0001 | 1000 |
| 3 | C (on), c (off) | 01.July.18 14:02:00;  3; 1 | [a0, B0, C1, c3] | (B0) | (C1) (c3) | (a0) |
| | | 01.July.18 16:03:00;  3; 0 | | $t_1$ | $t_2$   $t_3$ | $t_4$ |
| | | 01.July.18 16:00:01;  1; 0 | | Inputs | | Output |

**Fig. 2.** Configuration of LSTM network.

and 20% for testing). We investigate the dependence of the accuracy on the size of the dataset used for the complete process of training, validating, and testing the models. Prior to this, the optimum number of previous events to base the prediction of the next event on is found for each of the methods [7]. The accuracy results are computed within the testing set using the optimal memory length for each method. Figure 3 shows the results when the algorithms are applied to a dataset from a single apartment. A peak accuracy of 83% was achieved by LSTM with SPEED-text, while the SPEED algorithm achieved a peak accuracy of 82%. The accuracy achieved by the LSTM with ALZ-text was considerably lower at 69%. In this case, stability is achieved much later than with the other methods. Finally, the ALZ method reached a top accuracy of 70% with 4 weeks of data. Note that the probabilistic methods attain a good accuracy (close to the peak accuracy) with only 2 days of data. By comparison, the LSTM networks need approximately 2–3 weeks of data to start approaching their top accuracy. This indicates that the LSTM can learn longer term patterns and dependencies, and attain better accuracy based on these. In addition, LSTM networks needed much shorter time to train than SPEED - eight times faster.

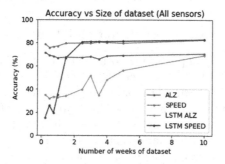

**Fig. 3.** Accuracy vs. size of dataset for all algorithms.

Subsequently, we develop the model further by using the time information in the best method – LSTM with SPEED-text. Here, the LSTM network was trained based on a 3-fold cross-validation. We use in total 40 weeks with recorded data from one apartment where we apply our algorithms, which accounts for 163347 events. Some accuracy curves do not show significant improvement after a certain number of events, and we therefore show the plots up to a certain point for better clarity on the lower range of the graph.

Firstly, we predict the next sensor event based on the two proposed input sequences with the time information (Sect. 4.2). Figure 4 shows the performance of the prediction vs. the amount of data in the dataset. When we include the time information in the input, the accuracy is improved by 1–1.4% for all methods as compared to Fig. 3. The highest accuracy (84.39%) is achieved by the 4-class time-interval. The small improvement compared to the best results from Fig. 3, was initially somewhat surprising, however, it can be explained by the fact that the apartments are quite small and there is a limited number of sensors and alternative sequences. The choice of 4- or 8-class time-interval classes does not have a significant effect on the accuracy. This is presumably because most of the events have a short elapsed time to the next event.

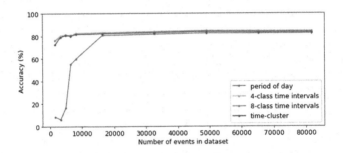

**Fig. 4.** Accuracy of prediction of next sensor event vs. the number of events in the dataset.

### 4.5   Prediction of Next Sensor Event and Time of Occurrence

We examine the accuracy of predicting both the next sensor event and time information using 4- and 8-class time-intervals or the K-means time-cluster. Lower accuracies are attained than when predicting only the next sensor event, as expected, since now more information is being predicted with the same model. The best accuracy was achieved by the K-means time-cluster (79.68%), 4% better than the second best-performing method (Fig. 5). The required number of events in the dataset is similar for the three methods, about 10000 events.

### 4.6   Transfer Learning Between Apartments

As described in Sect. 3, some power and magnetic sensors differ within the five apartments. In order to transfer the learning across the apartments, we re-label the sensors that refer to the same activity. Lamp power sensor events were removed from the datasets since we did not manage to assign them to an activity that was common for all lamps and apartments. In all cases, the LSTM network

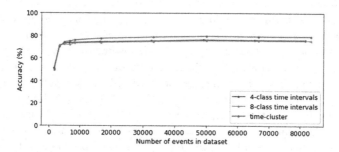

**Fig. 5.** Accuracy of prediction of next sensor event and time information vs. the number of events in the dataset.

was trained based on a certain number of events and tested on a test set containing 3000 events. This process is repeated three times and the accuracy values in the graph correspond to the mean of the best test accuracy of each training. Figure 6b presents the accuracy results when transfer learning is carried out as follows. The model is trained using data from four apartments and fine-tuned with and tested on the target apartment. A very low number of events is required for the fine-tuning to achieve quite high accuracy straight away. The accuracy increases slowly as more events are added for the fine-tuning.

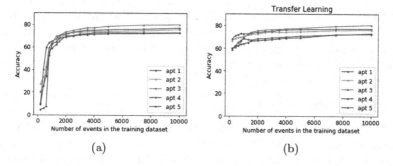

**Fig. 6.** Accuracy of prediction of the next sensor and time-cluster vs. number of events in the training dataset, using as input both sensor event and time-cluster, (a) separately for each apartment, (b) transfer learning, training the model with data from four apartments, fine-tuning with and testing on the target apartment.

# 5   Activity Recognition Using Depth Video Data

## 5.1   Data Preprocessing

Median filtering is applied to the raw depth video data to remove noise. The process consists of removing very low and very high pixel values in the image and replacing them with the median value of the nearest neighbors. A $5 \times 5$ filter was applied to each frame, as a compromise between image sharpness (quality) and its high frequency background noise. After this first step, we apply an Infinite Impulse Response (IIR) filter. The filter is configured as a first-order high pass in this work, which leads to capturing any movement. Finally, a last processing step is performed in order to normalize the length $n_i$ of frames of the video samples to a fixed length $N$, as this is a prerequisite for the convLSTM model. Frames are deleted if the sequence is shorter than N, or inserted if the sequence is longer than $N$. In both cases this takes place in equally spaced positions in the sequence (in accordance with the number of frames that need to be deleted/inserted), $n_i = N$. The value of each pixel in the inserted frames is equal to the mean between the preceding and succeeding frames. We use a convolutional long short-term memory network (convLSTM) for the classification. Convolutional neural networks (CNNs) have been widely used to process multiple arrays of data, including color or depth images. By combining CNNs with RNNs, the model is able to learn both spatial and temporal features from a sequence of frames [19].

In this work, the preprocessed and IIR-filtered frame sequences were labelled into four movement categories: TV-related movements (turn it on/off and switch over channels), standing up, sitting down and no movement. After the preprocessing, the sequences were fed to a convLSTM. The first two steps were implemented by using the median and IIR filters from the SciPy library. The convLSTM was implemented using the Keras library. The trained model comprises one convLSTM layer with three $3 \times 3$ filters and hyperbolic tangent activation, followed by a dense layer with softmax activation. The batch size was 16 and learning rate 0.01. Optimization function Adam and loss function categorical cross-entropy were optimal. We set the dropout ratio to 0.5 in order to avoid overfitting, as well as early stopping.

## 5.2  Activity Recognition

A total of 800 video sequences (200 of each category) were extracted from recordings acquired from real homes, from seven different residents. Each video sequence is length normalized to a size of 100 frames. We split our dataset into training (80%) and testing (20%) sets. They are both balanced for all classes (i.e. equal percentage of samples per class in each set).

We analyze the test accuracy attained for different sizes of datasets for two cases: only median filter, and both median and IIR filter. The obtained results correspond to an average of the three best accuracies achieved by different trained models – shuffling the training and testing data. The use of the IIR filter resulted in a best average peak accuracy of 86.04%, whereas by comparison without the IIR filter the best average peak accuracy achieved was 82.50%. Using the IIR filter improves the accuracy by approximately 4%, for all data sizes. The accuracy improves slowly as more samples are added, in both cases. The model did not reach stability with the available data, as the accuracy keeps increasing with data size. Hence better accuracy should be possible to achieve with additional samples. The confusion matrix is shown in Fig. 7.

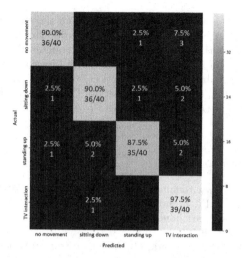

**Fig. 7.** Confusion matrix of model for 800 samples using both median and IIR filter.

# 6   Conclusion and Future Work

In this paper, we present work in progress, our field-trial and set-up for collecting and storing the data from real homes, and our results on activity recognition and prediction using either binary sensor data or depth video data. We compare the accuracy of predicting the next binary sensor event using probabilistic methods and LSTM networks. LSTM achieved the best accuracy of 83%. Using time information referring to the next sensor event improved this accuracy by 1.4%. Finally, we predicted both the next sensor event and its time of occurrence with a peak average accuracy of 80%. We have investigated transfer learning between apartments and shown that it is possible to pre-train the model with data from other apartments and achieve good accuracy straight away (70–80%) from the first day. The top accuracy in this case is similar to the one achieved when training each apartment individually.

We have in addition shown preliminary results from activity recognition using low resolution depth video data from seven apartments. 800 video samples were extracted containing four classes: no movement, standing up, sitting down, and TV interaction. We use a relatively simple processing method where we apply an IIR filter to extract movements from the frames prior to feeding them to a convLSTM network for the classification. We achieved an overall mean peak accuracy of 86%, with the accuracy of all classes reaching at least 85%. The method managed to identify TV-interaction actions with a peak accuracy of 97.5%. When the IIR filter is not used the accuracy is about 4–5% lower.

Future work will use state-of-the-art video processing techniques to carry out activity recognition and prediction in the homes, investigate data fusion combining binary data and depth video data, and carry out higher level activity recognition by utilizing movement and location information.

**Acknowledgement.** The authors would like to thank the residents and the house-keepers at the seniors' care unit Skøyen Omsorg+; Torhild Holthe and Dr. Anne Lund (OsloMet) for recruiting participants for the trial and communicating with the residents throughout the trial; Dejan Krunić and Øyvind Width (Sensio AS) for installations of the sensors; Oda Olsen Nedrejord and Wonho Lee (OsloMet) for contributions to the video data work; Prof. Jim Tørresen (University of Oslo) for valuable inputs; and the rest of the participants of the Assisted Living Project for a fruitful interdisciplinary collaboration.

# References

1. RoomMate. https://www.roommate.no/. Accessed 16 Nov 2018
2. Alam, M.R., Reaz, M.B., Mohd Ali, M.A.: SPEED: an inhabitant activity prediction algorithm for smart homes. IEEE Trans. Syst. Man Cybern. Part A Syst. Hum. **42**(4), 985–990 (2012)
3. Bataineh, K.M., Najia, M., Saqera, M.: A comparison study between various fuzzy clustering algorithms (2011)
4. Blackman, S., et al.: Ambient assisted living technologies for aging well: a scoping review. J. Intell. Syst. **25**(1), 55–69 (2016)
5. Box, G.E.P., Jenkins, G.: Time Series Analysis, Forecasting and Control. Holden-Day Inc., San Francisco (1990)
6. Casagrande, F.D., Tørresen, J., Zouganeli, E.: Sensor event prediction using recurrent neural network in smart homes for older adults. In: International Conference on Intelligent Systems (2018)
7. Casagrande, F.D., Tørresen, J., Zouganeli, E.: Comparison of probabilistic models and neural networks on prediction of home sensor events. In: Accepted at International Joint Conference on Neural Networks (2019)
8. Casagrande, F.D., Zouganeli, E.: Occupancy and daily activity event modelling in smart homes for older adults with mild cognitive impairment or dementia. In: Proceedings of the 59th Conference on Simulation and Modelling (SIMS 59), pp. 236–242 (2018)
9. Elhady, N.E., Provost, J.: A systematic survey on sensor failure detection and fault-tolerance in ambient assisted living. Sensors **18**(1991), 19 (2018)
10. Gopalratnam, K., Cook, D.J.: Online sequential prediction via incremental parsing: the active LeZi algorithm. IEEE Intell. Syst. **22**(1), 52–58 (2007)
11. Hochreiter, S., Schmidhuber, J.: Long short-term memory. Neural Comput. **9**(8), 1735–1780 (1997)
12. Joshi, K.D., Nalwade, P.S.: Modified k-means for better initial cluster centres (2013)
13. Lotfi, A., Langensiepen, C., Mahmoud, S.M., Akhlaghinia, M.J.: Smart homes for the elderly dementia sufferers: identification and prediction of abnormal behaviour. J. Ambient Intell. Humaniz. Comput. **3**(3), 205–218 (2012)
14. Mahmoud, S., Lotfi, A., Langensiepen, C.: Behavioural pattern identification and prediction in intelligent environments. Appl. Soft Comput. J. **13**(4), 1813–1822 (2013)
15. Mahmud, T., Hasan, M., Chakraborty, A., Roy-Chowdhury, A.K.: A Poisson process model for activity forecasting. In: 2016 IEEE International Conference on Image Processing (ICIP), pp. 3339–3343, September 2016
16. Minor, B., Cook, D.J.: Forecasting occurrences of activities. Pervasive Mob. Comput. (2016)

17. Nazerfard, E., Cook, D.J.: CRAFFT: an activity prediction model based on Bayesian networks. **33**(4), 395–401 (2015)
18. Reeder, B., Meyer, E., Lazar, A., Chaudhuri, S., Thompson, H.J., Demiris, G.: Framing the evidence for health smart homes and home-based consumer health technologies as a public health intervention for independent aging: a systematic review. Int. J. Med. Informatics **7**(82), 565–579 (2013)
19. Shi, X., Chen, Z., Wang, H., Yeung, D.Y., Wong, W.K., Woo, W.C.: Convolutional LSTM network: a machine learning approach for precipitation nowcasting (2015)
20. Wang, P., Li, W., Gao, Z., Zhang, J., Tang, C., Ogunbona, P.O.: Action recognition from depth maps using deep convolutional neural networks. IEEE Trans. Hum. Mach. Syst. **46**(4), 498–509 (2016)
21. Wu, S., et al.: Survey on prediction algorithms in smart homes. IEEE Internet Things J. **4**(3), 636–644 (2017)
22. Xia, L., Chen, C.C., Aggarwal, J.K.: View invariant human action recognition using histograms of 3D joints. In: IEEE Computer Society Conference on Computer Vision and Pattern Recognition Workshops, pp. 20–27. IEEE, June 2012
23. Yang, X., Zhang, C., Tian, Y.: Recognizing actions using depth motion maps-based histograms of oriented gradients. In: Proceedings of the 20th ACM International Conference on Multimedia - MM 2012, p. 1057 (2012)
24. Zhang, S., Wei, Z., Nie, J., Huang, L., Wang, S., Li, Z.: A review on human activity recognition using vision-based method. J. Healthc. Eng. **2017** (2017)
25. Zouganeli, E., et al.: Responsible development of self-learning assisted living technology for older adults with mild cognitive impairment or dementia. In: ICT4AWE 2017 - Proceedings of the 3rd International Conference on Information and Communication Technologies for Ageing Well and e-Health (ICT4AWE), pp. 204–209 (2017)

# Self-adapting Goals Allow Transfer of Predictive Models to New Tasks

Kai Olav Ellefsen[1(✉)] and Jim Torresen[2]

[1] Department of Informatics, University of Oslo, Oslo, Norway
kaiolae@ifi.uio.no
[2] Department of Informatics and RITMO, University of Oslo, Oslo, Norway

**Abstract.** A long-standing challenge in Reinforcement Learning is enabling agents to learn a model of their environment which can be transferred to solve other problems in a world with the same underlying rules. One reason this is difficult is the challenge of learning accurate models of an environment. If such a model is inaccurate, the agent's plans and actions will likely be sub-optimal, and likely lead to the wrong outcomes. Recent progress in model-based reinforcement learning has improved the ability for agents to learn and use predictive models. In this paper, we extend a recent deep learning architecture which learns a predictive model of the environment that aims to predict only the value of a few key measurements, which are indicative of an agent's performance. Predicting only a few measurements rather than the entire future state of an environment makes it more feasible to learn a valuable predictive model. We extend this predictive model with a small, evolving neural network that suggests the best goals to pursue in the current state. We demonstrate that this allows the predictive model to transfer to new scenarios where goals are different, and that the adaptive goals can even adjust agent behavior on-line, changing its strategy to fit the current context.

**Keywords:** Reinforcement Learning · Prediction · Neural networks · Neuroevolution

## 1 Introduction

Humans and animals rely on internal models (mental simulations of how objects respond to interaction) to predict the consequences of their actions and generate accurate motor commands in a wide range of situations [13,17]. Recent advances in deep learning have enabled computers to learn such predictive models by gathering a large collection of observations from an environment [9,16]. This opens up the possibility for guiding the actions of robots and computer agents by having them predict the consequences of each action and selecting the one leading to the best outcome.

When using predictions for guiding the actions of an agent, it is beneficial to limit the prediction to the most essential parts of the environment. For instance, if we would like to predict the effect of turning the steering wheel of a car, we should not try to predict the effect this has on birds we see in the sky,

© Springer Nature Switzerland AG 2019
K. Bach and M. Ruocco (Eds.): NAIS 2019, CCIS 1056, pp. 28–39, 2019.
https://doi.org/10.1007/978-3-030-35664-4_3

trees far away from us, and so on. Rather, we should focus on the effect on some key observable measurements, such as the car speed, and the distance to other cars and pedestrians. If we focus on predicting the parts of the environment we currently care about, the prediction problem becomes much more manageable.

This intuition is the background for a recent, popular technique for learning to act by predicting the future [2]. The technique makes the assumption that we can analyze the outcome of an action by focusing on *a few measurements*. These measurements should be the observable quantities that are most related to success or failure in some scenario. The authors propose that a way to learn how to act in an environment is to learn to predict the effect one's actions have on these measurements. Such predictions can readily be learned by gathering a large set of examples of observations, actions and resulting measurements from the environment (e.g. by simulating thousands of car trips).

Once one has learned to predict the measurements resulting from one's actions, it is possible to select the best action for a given situation, by choosing the one giving the *most optimal predicted measurements*. This requires some way to map the predicted future measurements to a number representing the *utility* of this future. [2] solved this by defining a goal vector, which weights the different measurements according to user-defined rules. For instance, a rule could be that we give a very high weight to the measurement of distance to the nearest pedestrian, and a lower positive weight to the measurement of car speed, reflecting that we want to drive efficiently, but only if pedestrians around us are safe.

In this paper, we explore the potential for *automatically adapting* such goal vectors to a given scenario (Fig. 1). We show that this allows the reuse of a learned predictive model in new situations, where the best strategy has changed. The automatically adapting goal vectors, together with the already learned predictive model, can quickly generate behaviors for new scenarios where the underlying rules are the same (allowing reuse of learned predictions), but the goals are different. We further show that our adaptive goal vectors can adapt agent strategies on-line, responding to changes as they occur.

## 2 Background

### 2.1 Model-Based Reinforcement Learning

The problems we target in this paper are reinforcement learning (RL) problems, meaning an agent is tasked with learning how to solve some problem without any explicit guidance – relying instead on infrequent feedback in the form of rewards and punishment from the environment. Reinforcement learning can be divided into two high-level categories: Model-based and model-free RL. Model-free RL means we try to solve the problem without forming an explicit model of the environment, relying instead on learning a mapping from observations to values or actions. Many of the recent successes in deep RL have been in this category, including deep Q learning [10], which was the first example of power of

(a) The Goal-ANN produces goals adapted to the current situation

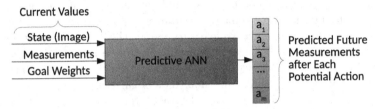

(b) The predictive ANN (developed by [2]) predicts the consequence of taking each action in the current situation.

**Fig. 1. Combining adaptive goals with prediction-based action selection.** Top: Our proposed Goal-ANN produces a weighting of the agent's goals adapted to the current situation (indicated by current measurements). Bottom: The resulting weights are given to the predictive ANN, together with the current state and current measurements, resulting in a vector of predicted future values for the measurements.

deep RL for playing computer games, and the deep deterministic policy gradient algorithm (DDPG) which demonstrated that deep neural networks can also learn to solve continuous control problems [8].

Model-based RL attempts to solve two key challenges with model-free approaches: (1) They require enormous amounts of training data, and (2) there is no straightforward way to transfer a learned policy to a new task in the same environment [12]. To do this, model-based RL takes the approach of first learning a predictive model of the environment, before using this model to make a plan that solves the problem. An internal predictive model facilitates transfer of knowledge to new tasks in the same environment: Once the predictions are learned, they can be used for planning ahead to solve many different tasks.

Despite these advantages of model-based algorithms, model-free RL has so far been most successful for complex environments. A key reason for this is that model based RL is likely to produce very bad policies if the learned predictive model is imperfect, which it will be for most complex environments [12]. Recently, algorithms have been developed which address this problem, for instance by learning to interpret imperfect predictions [12], applying new video prediction techniques [3] and dynamics models [4], or periodically restarting prediction sequences, reducing the effect of accuracy degrading for long-term prediction [5].

Another way to mitigate the problem of having an imperfect predictive model is to keep the prediction task as simple as possible. While the methods above generally try to predict the entire future state (more specifically, entire frames of input in the example of video games), one could predict more accurately by focusing on predicting exactly the values needed to guide action making. Dosovitskiy and Koltun [2] presented impressive results on the VizDoom RL environment by teaching agents to predict just a few key measurements, and combining this with a *goal vector* that defines a weighting among the measurements, effectively defining which type of future we most wish to observe. Here, we propose to combine this method with adaptive goal vectors, which has the potential to allow reuse of a predictive model in new scenarios where the goals are different.

## 2.2  Combining Deep Learning and Neuroevolution

Our proposed method combines two neural networks (Fig. 1), which are trained in different ways. The Prediction ANN is trained in a self-supervised manner, using the difference between predicted and actual future states as loss function. For the Goal-ANN, we have no target value, since we do not know the "correct" goal. We therefore optimize this networks by using neuroevolution, a technique employing a population of neural networks, having the ones performing their task best become further adapted and specialized to the problem [14].

A few other papers have recently combined deep learning with neuroevolution, aiming to get the benefits of both. Neuroevolution (NE) requires far more computation to solve problems than backpropagation-based deep learning. On the other hand, NE does not rely on a differentiable architecture, and works well in problems with sparse rewards, which are a challenge for most deep reinforcement learning algorithms [11]. A promising way to combine NE and DL is therefore to let the deep learning do the "heavy lifting", for instance learning to make predictions or recognize objects based on a large number of examples, and train a small action-selection component using NE with the pre-trained deep neural network as a back-end. This approach was taken by [3], who trained a self-supervised deep neural network to predict the future, and then evolved a much smaller network for selecting actions based on internal states in the predictive network. A similar idea is to train a convolutional neural network to translate raw pixels to compact feature representations, before training a smaller evolving ANN to use the learned features to choose the right actions in an RL problem. This has been done successfully for simulated car racing [7], for learning to aim and shoot in a video game [11] and for a health-gathering VizDoom scenario [1].

Similarly to the work described above, our method lets the DL component do the data-intensive job, which is to learn to predict the consequences of actions from a large number of examples. Unlike the methods above, we only require our deep network to predict a few key future measurements, greatly simplifying its task, and potentially reducing the impact of errors due to faulty predictions.

# 3  Methods

## 3.1  Learning to Act by Predicting the Future

The algorithm we propose in this paper is an extension of "Direct Future Prediction" (DFP) from the paper *Learning to act by predicting the future* [2]. DFP is based on the idea of transforming an RL problem into a self-supervised learning problem of predicting parts of future states and selecting actions that produce those states that align best with an agent's goals. A deep neural network is trained to predict the future value of a set of different measurements, $m$, given the current state and action. $m$ should contain metrics that give an indication of how successfully an agent is solving its task. The scenario explored here and in [2] is a video game where an agent attempts to survive and kill monsters. $m$ therefore contains measurements of an agent's ammunition, health and the number of enemies killed, which are all interesting indicators of an agent's performance.

If an agent can learn a model of how its actions affect future measurements, selecting the best action is reduced to a problem of finding which of the potential future $m$-vectors correspond best with the agent's goals. [2] solve this by formulating a goal-vector $g$, where each element indicates how much we care about the corresponding measurement in $m$. For instance, given that we use ammunition, health and enemies killed as measurements, the goal-vector $[0.5, 1, -1]$ would indicate that we are interested in collecting ammunition, twice as interested in collecting health, and interested in *avoiding* attacking enemies (due to the negative value for that goal).

Training this network to predict the effect of one's actions can now be done by collecting many episodes of gameplay, storing at each timestep $t$ current measurements $(m_t)$, sensory input $(s_t$ – frames of images from gameplay in this case), the action taken $(a_t)$ and the goal vector $(g_t$ – this is not changed during an episode while training). A sample of $(s_t, m_t, a_t, g_t)$ would now be the training input $(I)$, while the target output value $(O)$ would be the change in the measurements at selected future timesteps $(m_{t+\tau_1}, ..., m_{t+\tau_n})$. The network is trained using backpropagation with the loss function depending on the difference between its predicted change in future measurements $(\hat{O})$ and the actual observed values $(O)$.

## 3.2   Adaptive Goals Guiding Action Selection

The contribution of this paper is a technique for adapting the goals $(g)$ of DFP-agents, which enables them to (1) transfer predictive models to new tasks and (2) adjust goals on-line according to current measurements. To do so, we take a pre-trained predictive model from the DFP-algorithm, and extend it with an additional neural network that suggests the best goal-vector given the current measurements (Fig. 1).

This Goal-ANN is trained using neuroevolution [14]: A population of neural networks compete for their ability to produce relevant goals. The best networks are randomly changed, by adding or removing nodes and connections, while worse networks are discarded. To select between networks, they are each assigned a *fitness score* reflecting how well they perform their task. In our setup, we calculate the fitness by inserting the agent governed by the evaluated Goal-ANN and the (pre-trained) Predictive ANN into the game scenario, and measuring how well it performs its task (which varies slightly between our different experiments – see Sect. 4). To counter effects of randomness, each evaluation tests the agent 8 times and calculates the average performance.

The evolving networks are relatively small feed-forward ANNs where the connectivity and number of neurons are being optimized. The inputs are the 3 measurements $(m_t)$, and the output is the goal vector $(g_t)$ with the 3 corresponding goal weights. The inputs give the current value for the amount of ammunition, health and number of enemy kills (in that order), and the outputs represent the weight of the ammunition-objective, the health-objective, and the killing monsters-objective, all in the range $[-1, 1]$.

Our setup uses the popular neuroevolution algorithm NEAT [15], more specifically the NEAT-Python implementation[1], with the parameters shown in Table 1. With these parameters, each run of the algorithm results in 5,000 evaluations, corresponding to 5,000 1-min episodes of game play. The original DFP-algorithm was trained for around 95,000 episodes, demonstrating that our proposed goal-adaptation is an order of magnitude faster than training new strategies from scratch.

**Table 1.** Parameters for Python-NEAT

| Parameter | Value | | Parameter | Value |
|---|---|---|---|---|
| Add Connections | 0.15 | | Population Size | 50 |
| Delete Connection | 0.1 | | Generations | 100 |
| Add Node | 0.15 | | ANN Inputs / Outputs | 3 / 3 |
| Delete Node | 0.1 | | Weights Range | [-30, 30] |
| Weight Mutation | 0.8 | | Activation Function | Clamped linear response in range [-1,1] |
| Weight Replacement | 0.02 | | | |

(a) Mutation Rates

(b) Other parameters

### 3.3 Training Scenario

The scenario we use for training and testing the Goal-ANN is from the original paper suggesting DFP [2]. The scenario is based on the VizDoom platform [6], a popular platform for developing and testing reinforcement learning algorithms. VizDoom is based on the first-person shooter (FPS) Doom, and offers the potential to train agents to handle complex 3D environments directly from pixel inputs. VizDoom scenarios can be used to train and test skills such as understanding one's surroundings, navigation, exploration and dealing with opponents/enemies. The violent nature of the game is a concern, and we are eager to test our technique on more peaceful scenarios soon. However, to test extending the exact model trained in [2], we needed to reuse one of their scenarios.

---

[1] https://neat-python.readthedocs.io/.

The specific VizDoom scenario we use here is the one titled "D3-Battle" in [2]. This is a challenging scenario where the agent is under attack by alien monsters inside a maze, and has to try to kill as many of the monsters as possible. To aid the agent, ammunition and health kits are scattered around the maze. The agent is provided with (and learns to predict) three measurements: Its current amount of ammunition and health, as well as how many enemies it has killed. We use a trained predictive model from the original paper, which was trained in a "goal-agnostic" manner, that is, the goal vector $g$ was randomized between episodes (each value uniformly sampled from the interval $[-1, 1]$). Such goal-agnostic training was found to generalize better to new tasks than fixed-goal predictors [2], and we therefore focus on this model for our study.

## 4    Results

We want to explore two possible advantages of evolved goal weights: (1) Their ability to adapt an existing predictive model to new scenarios where strategies need to be different, and (2) Their ability to produce context-dependent goals, that is, goals that vary depending on current measurements.

To do so, we compare three main techniques: (1) Acting by following the same static goal-vector applied in [2], (2) Acting by following a simple rule for adapting the goal to the current situation and (3) Acting by following the evolved Goal-ANN. The static goal vector from [2] is $[0.5, 0.5, 1.0]$ where the three numbers represent the importance of the ammunition-, health- and enemy kills-objectives, respectively. This goal captures the intuition that the aim of the game is to kill as many monsters as possible, but collecting some ammunition and health is a good side-goal to help the agent in its primary mission. The simple rule to improve this static goal (called "Hardcoded" in plots below) is to switch to the goal $[0, 1.0, -1.0]$ whenever the agent's health is below 50%, which adds the intuition that we should stop attacking and focus on gathering health when injured.

In all plots below, fitness values are averaged over 20 independent evaluations of each agent.

### 4.1    The Original Scenario

As mentioned above, we test our method on a VizDoom scenario developed by [2], using their pre-trained agent together with our evolved adaptive goals. The scenario consists of a maze populated by monsters and the agent. The goal of the trained agent is to kill as many monsters as possible, and to do so, it can benefit from collecting ammunition and health packages along the way. In this original scenario, the final reward (also referred to as Fitness below, as is common in Evolutionary Algorithms) is based only on the number of monsters killed.

Figure 2 shows the average reward (number of monsters killed in one minute) of the three compared techniques on the original scenario. There are no significant differences between the compared techniques. In other words, there is no advantage to adapting the goals in this scenario.

Analyzing the agents' gameplay in this scenario reveals why this is the case: Agents are very fast, killing monsters without taking much damage, which makes the default goal of aggressively attacking monsters while picking up any health or ammo ahead a very good choice. In other words, there is no conflict among the goals and no reason why a different choice of goal weights should improve performance.

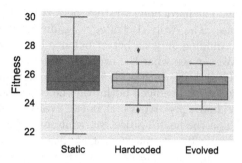

**Fig. 2. The original scenario.** No significant differences in fitness values between using the original goal (Static), a simple adaptive goal (Hardcoded) and the evolved Goal-ANN.

### 4.2 A Hard Scenario

To test the ability of the adaptive goals to solve different scenarios, and the potential for adjusting goals during gameplay, we set up a much harder scenario. We introduce the following difficulties that force the agent to sometimes change its strategy between defensive and aggressive modes:

- Monsters are tougher (they have twice as much health as before).
- Player is weaker (it begins the game with only 10% health)
- A fitness penalty of 100 is given for dying (versus 0 before).
- Player starts with 0 initial ammunition (versus 20 bullets before).

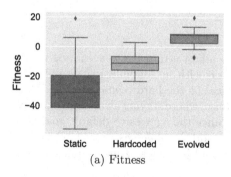

(a) Fitness

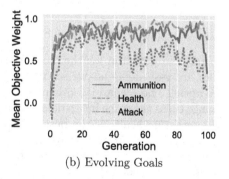

(b) Evolving Goals

**Fig. 3. The hard scenario.** Left: The evolved adaptive Goal-ANN significantly outperforms both the standard (static) and hardcoded (dynamic) goals. Right: The mean population value for each goal through evolution. The evolved strategies tend to focus more on health and less on attacking.

Since the monsters are now stronger and the player weaker, the default static goals result in a strategy that is too aggressive and frequently results in the player dying. The hardcoded strategy performs better, since it balances aggression and defense. The evolved strategy significantly outperforms both the others ($p < 0.05$), finding an even better balance between the three objectives (Fig. 3a).

We can see what the evolved strategy has learned by plotting the output of the Goal-ANN. In Fig. 3b we plot the output of the Goal-ANN per generation of evolution, averaged both over the entire population and all timesteps in each individual's life. We see that the evolved strategies gradually move towards a focus on the health-objective, while reducing focus on attacking enemies.

Figure 3b summarizes strategies over complete game episodes. However, the Goal-ANN has the potential to produce strategies that vary through a game, depending on the current measurements. To investigate if this is taking place, we performed a sweep over sensible values for all three measurements, passed these values through the best evolved Goal-ANN and measured the resulting output goals. The results show that changing the current health or the number of kills has no effect on the produced goals. However, changing the amount of ammunition does

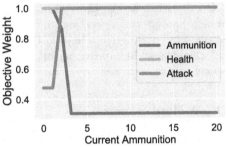

**Fig. 4. The hard scenario.** The strategy discovered by evolution is to focus on gathering ammunition until some has been collected, after which the agent switches to attacking. Simultaneously, the agent focuses on collecting health.

affect the output goals, as plotted in Fig. 4. We see that evolution has discovered the strategy of focusing less on attacking and more on gathering ammunition when the current ammunition level is low[2].

### 4.3 The No-Ammunition Scenario

To test the potential for the Goal-ANN to adapt strategies to scenarios where rules are very different, we set up a scenario with no ammunition available to the agent. The scenario is otherwise identical to the hard scenario above. This change turns the game into a defensive exercise, where staying away from enemies and gathering health is the best strategy. Since the aggressive default goal now results in a very bad strategy, we here test an additional *defensive* goal, which has the maximum negative weight on the attack-objective, and maximum positive weights on the two others ($g = [1, 1, -1]$).

As expected, the default aggressive strategy performs very badly in this scenario, while the hardcoded and the new defensive strategy do better (Fig. 5a). The evolved strategy significantly outperforms all others, with $p < 0.01$ according to the Mann-Whitney U test, for all pairwise comparisons. We were initially surprised to see the evolved strategy outperform the defensive strategy, since

---

[2] https://youtu.be/NCzrO5KHMXQ shows an agent playing according to this strategy.

we expected its full focus on avoiding confrontation to be optimal. We therefore took a closer look at the evolved strategy[3].

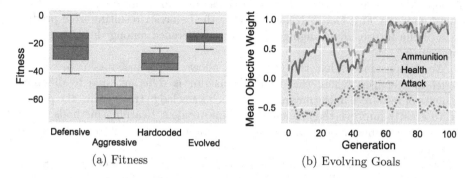

(a) Fitness                          (b) Evolving Goals

**Fig. 5. The scenario with no ammunition.** Left: Evolved adaptive goals generated by the Goal-ANN significantly outperform both the static (Aggressive and Defensive) and Hardcoded goals. Right: The mean population value for each goal through evolution. The evolved strategies quickly learn to not focus on attacking.

As expected, we found the evolving strategy to give a strong negative weight to the attack-objective, and strong positive weights to the two others (Fig. 5b). Repeating the sweep across measurements, we found that the current health measure is the only value that leads to different goals when changed. The evolved strategy is to focus exclusively on collecting health when the measure is critically low, and otherwise to also include a drive for collecting ammunition, in both cases avoiding attacking as strongly as

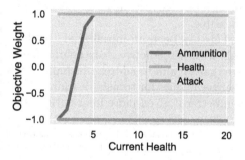

**Fig. 6. The scenario with no ammunition.** The strategy discovered by evolution is to focus on only on health if it is low, but add focus on gathering ammunition otherwise.

possible (Fig. 6). It may seem surprising that the ammunition objective is valuable at all here, since there is no ammunition in the environment. We hypothesize that a high value for this objective can be valuable, since it can encourage the agent to keep moving, heading towards objects with a small resemblance of ammunition, thus staying away from danger.

---

[3] https://youtu.be/6pTnkCGV6NI shows an agent playing according to this strategy.

# 5   Conclusion

We proposed extending an existing technique for selecting actions based on predictions of the consequences of those actions with an adaptive goal-producing neural network. This Goal-ANN can modify the behavior resulting from predictions of the future, by changing the agent's preference among different future outcomes.

We demonstrated that the Goal-ANN allows the transfer of a predictive model to scenarios where the optimal behavior is different, due to different amounts of resources in the environment. Such knowledge transfer has the potential to greatly improve the efficiency of Reinforcement Learning methods, since they allow training a model on one task, and adapting it rapidly to other, related problems.

We also showed that the Goal-ANN is capable of learning *adaptive* strategies, where goals change on-line, depending on the current state of the environment. This is a very valuable property, since most complex problems require one to modify one's strategy depending on the current context.

A final valuable feature of the Goal-ANN is its *interpretability*: We can easily probe the rules it has learned by sweeping across input measurements and observing the resulting output goals. We demonstrated that in our target scenarios, such an analysis allows us to verify that the learned goal-switching behavior is sensible.

This has been an initial study of the potential for combining self-adapting goals with a predictive deep neural network. There are many future questions here that we aim to address, including tests on more scenarios, comparison with other techniques for transfer learning and testing if the Goal-ANN could perform even better if given more information about the current state of the world.

**Acknowledgments.** This work is supported by The Research Council of Norway as part of the Engineering Predictability with Embodied Cognition (EPEC) project #240862, and the Centres of Excellence scheme, project #262762.

# References

1. Alvernaz, S., Togelius, J.: Autoencoder-augmented neuroevolution for visual doom playing. In: 2017 IEEE Conference on Computational Intelligence and Games (CIG) (2017)
2. Dosovitskiy, A., Koltun, V.: Learning to act by predicting the future. In: ICLR 2017, pp. 1–14 (2017)
3. Ha, D., Schmidhuber, J.: Recurrent world models facilitate policy evolution. In: Advances in Neural Information Processing Systems 31, pp. 2451–2463. Curran Associates, Inc. (2018)
4. Hafner, D., et al.: Learning latent dynamics for planning from pixels. arXiv preprint arXiv:1811.04551, November 2018
5. Kaiser, L., et al.: Model-based reinforcement learning for atari. arXiv preprint arXiv:1903.00374 (2019)

6. Kempka, M., Wydmuch, M., Runc, G., Toczek, J., Jaskowski, W.: ViZDoom: a doom-based AI research platform for visual reinforcement learning. In: IEEE Conference on Computational Intelligence and Games, CIG (2017)
7. Koutnik, J., Schmidhuber, J., Gomez, F.: Evolving deep unsupervised convolutional networks for vision-based reinforcement learning. In: Proceedings of the 2014 Annual Conference on Genetic and Evolutionary Computation, pp. 541–548. ACM (2014)
8. Lillicrap, T.P., et al.: Continuous control with deep reinforcement learning. arXiv preprint arXiv:1509.02971 (2015)
9. Luc, P., Neverova, N., Couprie, C., Verbeek, J., Lecun, Y.: Predicting deeper into the future of semantic segmentation. In: Proceedings of the IEEE International Conference on Computer Vision (2017)
10. Mnih, V., et al.: Human-level control through deep reinforcement learning. Nature **518**(7540), 529–533 (2015)
11. Poulsen, A.P., Thorhauge, M., Funch, M.H., Risi, S.: DLNE: a hybridization of deep learning and neuroevolution for visual control. In: 2017 IEEE Conference on Computational Intelligence and Games, CIG 2017 (2017)
12. Racanière, S., et al.: Imagination-augmented agents for deep reinforcement learning. In: Advances in Neural Information Processing Systems 30, pp. 5690–5701. Curran Associates, Inc. (2017)
13. Schillaci, G., Hafner, V.V., Lara, B.: Exploration behaviours, body representations and simulations processes for the development of cognition in artificial agents. Front. Robot. AI **3**, 39 (2016)
14. Stanley, K.O., Clune, J., Lehman, J., Miikkulainen, R.: Designing neural networks through neuroevolution. Nat. Mach. Intell. **1**(1), 24–35 (2019)
15. Stanley, K.O., Miikkulainen, R.: Evolving neural network through augmenting topologies. Evol. Comput. **10**(2), 99–127 (2002)
16. Villegas, R., Yang, J., Zou, Y., Sohn, S., Lin, X., Lee, H.: Learning to generate long-term future via hierarchical prediction. In: ICML, April 2017
17. Wolpert, D.M., Doya, K., Kawato, M.: A unifying computational framework for motor control and social interaction. Philos. Trans. R. Soc. B Biol. Sci. **358**(1431), 593–602 (2003)

# Autonomous Vehicle Control: End-to-End Learning in Simulated Urban Environments

Hege Haavaldsen⑩, Max Aasbø⑩, and Frank Lindseth$^{(\boxtimes)}$⑩

Norwegian University of Science and Technology, Trondheim, Norway
frankl@ntnu.no

**Abstract.** In recent years, considerable progress has been made towards a vehicle's ability to operate autonomously. An end-to-end approach attempts to achieve autonomous driving using a single, comprehensive software component. Recent breakthroughs in deep learning have significantly increased end-to-end systems' capabilities, and such systems are now considered a possible alternative to the current state-of-the-art solutions.

This paper examines end-to-end learning for autonomous vehicles in simulated urban environments containing other vehicles, traffic lights, and speed limits. Furthermore, the paper explores end-to-end systems' ability to execute navigational commands and examines whether improved performance can be achieved by utilizing temporal dependencies between subsequent visual cues.

Two end-to-end architectures are proposed: a traditional Convolutional Neural Network and an extended design combining a Convolutional Neural Network with a recurrent layer. The models are trained using expert driving data from a simulated urban setting, and are evaluated by their driving performance in an unseen simulated environment.

The results of this paper indicate that end-to-end systems can operate autonomously in simple urban environments. Moreover, it is found that the exploitation of temporal information in subsequent images enhances a system's ability to judge movement and distance.

**Keywords:** End-to-end learning · Imitation learning · Autonomous vehicle control · Artificial intelligence · Deep learning

## 1 Introduction

We are currently at the brink of a new paradigm in human travel: the fully autonomous, self-driving car. Only 50 years ago, cars were completely analog devices with almost no mechanisms for assisting the driver. Over the decades, additional features, controls, and technologies have been integrated, and cars have evolved into exceedingly complex machines.

H. Haavaldsen and M. Aasbø contributed equally to this work.

© Springer Nature Switzerland AG 2019
K. Bach and M. Ruocco (Eds.): NAIS 2019, CCIS 1056, pp. 40–51, 2019.
https://doi.org/10.1007/978-3-030-35664-4_4

In recent years, substantial progress has been made towards a vehicle's ability to operate autonomously. Primarily, two different approaches have emerged. The prevailing state of the art approach is to divide the problem into a number of sub-problems and solve them by combining techniques from computer vision, sensor fusion, localization, control theory, and path planning. This approach requires expert knowledge in several domains and often results in complex solutions, consisting of several cooperating modules.

Another approach is to develop an end-to-end solution, solving the problem using a single, comprehensive component, e.g., a deep neural network. A technique for training such a system is to employ imitation learning. This entails studying expert decisions in different scenarios, to find a mapping between the perceived environments and the executed actions. While some believe that the black-box characteristics of such systems makes them untrustworthy and unreliable, others point to recent years' advances in deep-learning and argue that end-to-end solutions show great potential.

However, end-to-end systems cannot make the correct navigational decision solely based on a perceived environment. It is also necessary to incorporate a user's intent in situations that require a decision (e.g., when approaching an intersection). Hence, an end-to-end system should be able to receive and adapt to navigational commands.

The objective of this paper is to investigate end-to-end systems' ability to drive autonomously in simulated urban environments. Specifically, to study their performance in environments containing other vehicles, traffic lights, and speed limits; to examine their ability to oblige navigational commands in intersections; and to explore if a system can improve its performance by utilizing temporal dependencies between subsequent visual cues.

This paper seeks to combine different aspects from recent research in the field of end-to-end learning for autonomous vehicles. Concretely, the use of navigational commands as network input, and the exploitation of temporal dependencies between subsequent images. There have been no attempts - to our knowledge - to combine both techniques in one system. Hopefully, this can lead to a more complete end-to-end system and improved driving quality.

The rest of this paper is organized as follows. Section 2 presents previous related work, while Sect. 3 addresses the environment in which the data was collected and the experiments were conducted. Section 4 reviews the collection and preprocessing of the data. The model architectures are presented in Sect. 5. Sections 6 and 7 covers the experimental setup and results, while Sect. 8 discusses the results. Finally, Sect. 9 covers the conclusions.

## 2   Related Work

There have been several advances in end-to-end learning for autonomous vehicles over the last decades. The first approach was seen already in 1989 when a fully connected neural network was used to control a vehicle [10]. In 2003 a proof-of-concept project called DAVE emerged [9], showing a radio controlled vehicle being able to drive around in a junk-filled alley and avoiding obstacles. DAVE truly showed the potential of an end-to-end approach. Three years later NVIDIA developed DAVE-2 [1], a framework with the objective to make real vehicles drive reliably on public roads. DAVE-2 is the basis for most end-to-end approaches seen today [2, 7]. The project used a CNN to predict a vehicle's steering commands. Their model was able to operate on roads with or without lane markings and other vehicles, as well as parking lots and unpaved roads.

Codevilla et al. [2] further explored NVIDIA's architecture by adding navigational commands to incorporate the drivers intent into the system and predicted both steering angle and acceleration. The authors proposed two network architectures: a *branched network* and a *command input network*. The *branched network* used the navigational input as a switch between a CNN and three fully connected networks, each specialized to a single intersection action, while the *command input network* concatenated the navigational command with the output of the CNN, connected to a single fully connected network.

Hubschneider et al. [7] proposed using turn signals as control commands to incorporate the steering commands into the network. Furthermore, they proposed a modified network architecture to improve driving accuracy. They used a CNN that receives an image and a turn indicator as input such that the model could be controlled in real time. To handle sharp turns and obstacles along the road the authors proposed using images recorded several meters back to obtain a spatial history of the environment. Images captured 4 and 8 m behind the current position were added as an input to make up for the limited vision from a single centered camera.

Eraqi et al. [4] tried to utilize the temporal dependencies by combining a CNN with a Long Short-Term Memory Neural Network. Their results showed that the C-LSTM improved the angle prediction accuracy by 35% and stability by 87%.

## 3   Environment

Training and testing models for autonomous driving in the physical world can be expensive, impractical, and potentially dangerous. Gathering a sufficient amount of training data requires both human resources and suitable hardware, and it can be time consuming to capture, organize and label the desired driving scenarios. Moreover, the cost of unexpected behavior while testing a model may be considerable.

An alternative is to train and test models in a simulated environment. A simulator can effectively provide a variety of corner cases needed for training, validation, and testing; while removing safety risks and material costs. Additionally, the labeling of the dataset can be automated, removing the cost of manual labeling, as well as the potential of human error.

The drawback, however, is the loss of realism. A simulation is only an imitation of a real-world system, and a model trained on only simulated data may not be able to function reliably in the real world. Nonetheless, a simulator can give a good indication of a model's actual driving performance and serves well for benchmarking different models. Once a model can perform reliably in a simulated environment, the model can be fine-tuned for further testing in real environments.

In this paper, the CARLA simulator [3] is used to gather training data and to evaluate the proposed models. CARLA is an open source simulator built for autonomous driving research and provides an urban driving environment populated with buildings, vehicles, pedestrians, and intersections.

# 4    Data Generation

## 4.1    Data Collection

When performing imitation learning, the quality of the training data plays a significant role in a model's ability to perform reliably in different conditions. However, a model trained only using expert data in ideal environments may not learn how to recover from perturbations. To overcome this, several types of driving data was captured. Expert driving was captured using CARLA's built-in autopilot, resulting in center-of-lane driving while following speed-limits. To capture more volatile data, a randomly generated noise value was added to the autopilot's outgoing control signal. This resulted in sudden shifts in the vehicle's trajectory and speed, which the autopilot subsequently tried to correct. To eliminate undesirable behavior in the training set, only the autopilot's response to the noise was collected, not the noisy control signal. Finally, recovery from possible disaster states was captured by manually steering the vehicle into undesired locations, e.g., the opposite lane, or the sidewalk; while recording the recovery.

For each recorded frame, images from three forward-facing cameras (positioned at the left, center, and right side of the vehicle) were captured, along with the vehicle's control signal (i.e., steering angle, throttle, and brake values), and additional information (i.e., speed, speed limit, traffic light state, and *High-Level Command*). The *High-Level Command* (HLC) is the active navigational command, labeling the data with the user's current intent. Possible HLCs are: *follow lane, turn left at the next intersection, turn right at the next intersection,* and *continue straight ahead at the next intersection.*

Two different datasets were gathered, one for training and one for testing. The training set was captured in CARLA's Town 1, while the test set was captured in Town 2. Data were gathered in four different weather conditions: Clear noon, cloudy noon, clear sunset, and cloudy sunset. The training set contained driving data captured both with and without other vehicles. The test set exclusively contained driving data alongside other vehicles. All data were captured in environments without pedestrians. Table 1 summarizes the gathered datasets. All expert data was captured driving 10 km/h below the speed limit to match the velocity of other vehicles.

**Table 1.** The collected datasets. An observation contains the captured data from a single rendered frame in the simulator.

| Dataset | Number of observations | Size [GB] |
|---|---|---|
| Training | 117 889 | 31.5 |
| Testing | 23 173 | 8.32 |

### 4.2  Data Preparation

For each recorded observation, a data sample was created containing the center image, the vehicle's control signal, and the additional information. Moreover, to simulate the recovery from drifting out of the lane, two new data samples were generated using the observation's left and right images. To counteract the left and right images' positional offset, the associated steering angle was shifted by +0.1 and −0.1 respectively.

For each data sample, a new augmented sample was generated using one of the desirable transformations picked at random. These included a random change in brightness or contrast, the addition of Gaussian noise or blur, and the addition of randomly generated dark polygons differing in position and shape.

When recording the datasets, the majority of the observations were captured driving straight. To prevent an unbalanced dataset, data samples with a small steering angle were downsampled (by removal), while data samples with a large steering angle were upsampled (by duplication). Additionally, the data samples corresponding to the different intersection decisions (i.e., turn left, turn right, or straight ahead) were balanced by analyzing the distributions of HLC-properties in the dataset and downsampling the over-represented choices. Finally, some of the data samples where the vehicle was not moving (e.g., waiting for a red light) were downsampled.

## 5    Model Architectures

In this paper, two related end-to-end architectures are proposed. The first is a Convolutional Neural Network (CNN) inspired by NVIDIA's DAVE-2 [1] system, while the second extends the CNN with Long-Short-Term-Memory (LSTM) units to capture temporal dynamic behavior.

### 5.1  CNN Model

The CNN model consists of two connected modules: a feature extractor and a prediction module. The former uses a CNN to extract useful features from the input image, while the latter combines the detected features with the additional inputs (i.e., current speed, speed limit, traffic light state, and HLC) to predict a control signal (i.e., steering angle, throttle and brake values).

The convolutional part of the model is inspired by the architecture used in NVIDIA's DAVE-2 system [1]. The modified network takes a $180 \times 300 \times 3$ image as input, followed by a cropping layer and a normalization layer. The cropping layer removes the top 70 pixels from the image, while the normalization layer scales the pixel values between $-0.5$ and $0.5$. Next follows six convolutional layers, all using a ReLU activation function. The first three layers use a $5 \times 5$ filter, while the last three use a $3 \times 3$ filter. The first four layers use a stride of 2, while the last two use a stride of 1. The output of the last convolutional layer is flattened resulting in a one-dimensional feature layer containing 768 nodes.

The output from the convolutional layers is concatenated with the additional input containing the speed, speed-limit, traffic-sign, and HLC values. The concatenated layer serves as an input for the predictive part of the model which consists of three dense layers containing 100, 50, 10 nodes respectively. All the dense layers use a ReLU activation function. The last of the dense layers are finally connected to an output layer, consisting of 3 nodes. The complete architecture is shown in Fig. 1.

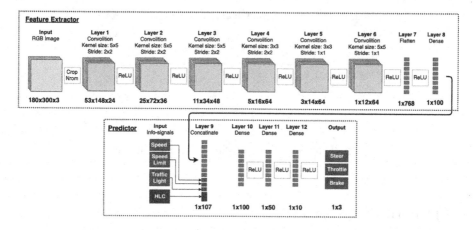

**Fig. 1.** The architecture of the CNN model. The model accepts a single RGB image and predicts a control signal.

## 5.2   CNN-LSTM Model

The CNN-LSTM model consists of two connected modules: a feature extractor and a temporal prediction module. The former follows the same architecture as the previous model, shown in Fig. 1. The feature extractor is connected to an LSTM layer with 5 hidden states. The model uses a sequence of feature extractions over time to predict a control signal. This allows the model to learn temporal dependencies between time steps.

For each time step, the output of the feature extractor is concatenated with the additional input containing speed, speed limit, traffic light, and an HLC. This is sent through a dense layer containing 100 nodes and fed into an LSTM layer with 10 nodes. For each time step in the sequence, the LSTM layer sends its output to itself. At the last time step, the output is sent through a dense layer, consisting of three nodes. This is the final prediction. The complete architecture is shown in Fig. 2.

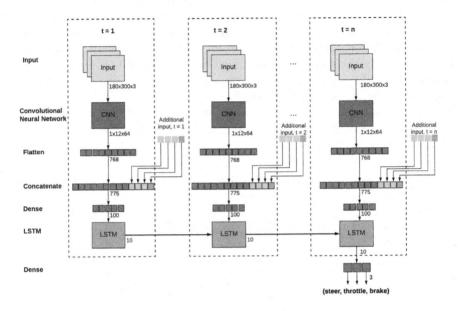

**Fig. 2.** The architecture of the CNN-LSTM model.

# 6 Experimental Setup

## 6.1 Training

**Training and Validation.** The dataset was split into a training set (70%) and a validation set (30%).

For the CNN-LSTM, the data samples were further structured into sequences of length five, using a sampling interval of three. The sequence length determines the number of time steps the LSTM layer is able to remember, while the sampling interval decides the period between successive individual time steps within the sequences. Figure 3 illustrates the structuring of sequences from 15 data samples.

**Hyperparameters.** Both models were trained using an Adam optimizer [8] and an Mean Squared Error loss function. The models were trained for a 100 epochs, with a batch size of 32 data-samples. The models' weights were recorded after each epoch along with the associated validation error. After the training was complete, the weights associated with the lowest validation error were chosen for further testing.

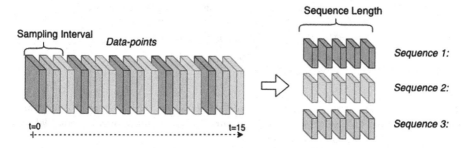

**Fig. 3.** The structuring of sequences from an array of data samples. A sequence length of five and a sampling interval of three is used.

## 6.2   Testing

After training, each model's predictive and real-time performance was measured. The predictive performance was tested by exposing the models to the unseen test set while calculating the average prediction error. The real-time performance was tested by letting the models control a simulated vehicle in CARLA's second town. Each model was to drive through a predefined route ten times. The test evaluator provided HLCs to the model before each intersection. A model's performance was measured in the number of route completions, the average route completion percentage, and the number of failures. Model failures were recorded according to severity. Touching a lane line was considered a minor failure, while a low-speed rear-ending or an object collision was considered a moderate failure. Object collisions without recovery or an ignored HLC were considered a severe failure. Catastrophic failures consisted of either entering the opposite lane, disregarding a red traffic light, or colliding with oncoming traffic.

## 7   Experimental Results

### 7.1   Validation and Test Error

After 100 epochs of training, both models' training and validation loss had stabilized. The CNN and CNN-LSTM had their lowest validation error after epoch 66 and 81 respectively. The models were then evaluated on the unseen test set from CARLA's second town. On the test set, the CNN was able to predict a control signal with an average error of 0.023, a 43% increase compared to its validation error. The CNN-LSTM was able to predict a control signal with an average error of 0.022, a 57% increase compared to its validation error (Table 2).

### 7.2   Real-Time Test in Simulated Environment

Both models were real-time tested in CARLA's second town. To test their ability to handle various driving scenarios in an urban environment, each model drove a predefined route ten times. The results are described below. Two videos were

**Table 2.** Test and validation loss during the training of the models.

| Model | Validation loss | Test loss |
|---|---|---|
| CNN | 0.016 | 0.023 |
| CNN-LSTM | 0.014 | 0.022 |

**Table 3.** Summary of test results. Each model attempted to drive a predefined route ten times. A model's performance were measured in the number of route completions and the average route completion percentage.

| Model | Route completions | Avg. route completion |
|---|---|---|
| CNN | 2 | 56% ± 39 |
| CNN-LSTM | 5 | 81% ± 9 |

**Table 4.** Average failures per run. The models' failures were recorded according to severity. Touching a lane line was considered a minor failure, while a low-speed rear-ending or an object collision was considered a moderate failure. Object collisions without recovery or an ignored HLC were considered a severe failure. A catastrophic failure consisted of either entering the opposite lane, disregarding a red traffic light, or colliding with oncoming traffic.

| Model | Minor | Moderate | Severe | Catastrophic |
|---|---|---|---|---|
| CNN | 2.10 ± 1.73 | 0.65 ± 0.99 | 0.25 ± 0.44 | 0.23 ± 0.57 |
| CNN-LSTM | 2.90 ± 1.72 | 0.10 ± 0.31 | 0.05 ± 0.22 | 0.17 ± 0.38 |

created to show a successful run and some common failures. One demonstrates the CNN model [5] and the other demonstrates the CNN-LSTM model [6].

**CNN.** Out of ten runs, the CNN model was able to complete the predefined route twice, with an average completion percentage of 56% over all runs. The model performed well on lane following and drove reliably in the center of the lane most of the time. The model handled most intersections but had a tendency to perform very sharp right turns. This resulted in 2.1 minor failures (i.e., the vehicle touching the lane line) per run. It always tried to follow the provided HLC, and never ignored a traffic light. It was able to handle complex light conditions, such as direct sunlight and dark shadows in the road. The model hit objects without recovery several times, leading to 0.5 severe failures per run. The vehicle rarely hit objects outside of the lane, but occasionally struggled to stop for other vehicles, leading to several low speed rear-end collisions. In total, the model had 0.1 object collisions, and 1.2 rear-end collisions per run. Finally, 0.7 times per run it struggled to find the lane after a turn, leading to a catastrophic failure. The model usually held the speed limit but found it hard to slow down fast enough to a speed limit when the speed was high. The results are summarized in Tables 3 and 4.

**CNN-LSTM.** The CNN-LSTM model was able to complete the predefined route five out of ten times, with an average completion percentage of 81% over all runs. It drove reliably in the center of the lane most of the time but tended to perform sharp turns. This lead to 2.9 minor failures (i.e., lane line touches) per run. The model always tried to follow the provided HLC, and never ignored a traffic light. It managed to handle various light conditions, such as direct sunlight and dark shadows in the road. The vehicle rarely struggled to stop for other objects or vehicles, resulting in 0.1 object collisions and 0.1 rear-end collisions per run. Finally, 0.5 times per run it struggled to find the lane after a turn, leading to a catastrophic failure. The model adapted well to the different speed limits. The results are summarized in Tables 3 and 4.

## 8  Discussion

This paper proposed two architectures for an end-to-end system: a traditional CNN inspired by NVIDIA's DAVE-2 system [1], and an extended design combining the CNN with an LSTM layer to facilitate learning of temporal relationships. Both models were able to follow a lane consistently and reliably. Any disturbances or shifts in the trajectory were quickly corrected, without being overly sensitive. The CNN exhibited less volatile steering compared to the CNN-LSTM in the high-speed stretch of the route, but the CNN-LSTM outperformed the CNN in turns following high-speed stretches. Additionally, both models obeyed all traffic lights and always tried to follow the provided HLC at intersections.

When introducing other vehicles, the differences between the models became more apparent. The CNN-LSTM adapted its speed according to traffic, and only rear-ended another vehicle once throughout the whole experiment. In scenarios where another vehicle blocked most of the view (e.g., when following another vehicle closely in a turn), the CNN-LSTM seemed to be able to use past predictions as a guide. The CNN, on the other hand, experienced more trouble when driving alongside other vehicles. Although the model, to some degree, adapted its speed according to traffic, it often failed to react upon sudden changes. This led to frequent rear-endings throughout the experiment.

The difference between the models' performance may be explained in their architectural differences. The CNN-LSTM model used five subsequent observations when making predictions. This allowed it, by all indication, to learn some important temporal dependencies - acquiring some knowledge about the relationships between movement, change in object size, and distance. The CNN model, however, interpreted each observation independently, which restrained its ability to understand motion. It still learned to brake when approaching a vehicle, but was not able to differentiate between fast approaching and slow approaching objects. Predictions related to distance were solely dependent on the size of objects. Moreover, the CNN could not rely on past predictions when faced with confusing input, which seemed to result in more unreliable behavior.

It should be mentioned that although the CNN model had 28% less minor failures than the CNN-LSTM model, its completion rate was 32% lower than the CNN-LSTM. The reduction in minor failures was probably a result of the lower average route completion, not an indication of better performance.

## 8.1  Consistency with Related Work

The implemented models in this paper are based on the architecture in [1]. The authors were able to use a CNN to drive on trafficked roads with and without lane markings, parking lots and unpaved roads. This complies with this paper's results. Even though the implemented models were not tested on unmarked roads or parking lost, they were able to drive on roads with lane marking, both on roads with and without pavements.

Codevilla et al. [2] claimed that their *command input network* performed inadequately when executing navigational commands. This does not comply with the results of this paper. The proposed architecture takes the navigational command as input after the CNN, in a similar matter to the *command input network*, but was able to execute the given navigational commands with a high degree of success.

In [7] the turn indicators of the car was used as the navigational commands, which were sent as input to the network. The authors did not use an RNN, but fed three subsequent images to three CNNs and concatenated the output. It was able to perform lane following, avoid obstacles and change lanes. The navigational commands in this paper were introduced to the network in a similar way, and both approaches were able to execute the navigational commands. The proposed system was not tested for lane changes, but seeing achievements in similar approaches indicates that this should be possible.

The CNN model in this paper was extended with an LSTM to utilize temporal dependencies. A similar approach was attempted in [4]. They showed that adding temporal dependencies improved both the accuracy and stability of a model using a single CNN. Similar results can be seen in this paper.

## 9  Conclusion

The results of the experiments indicates that end-to-end systems are able to operate autonomously in simulated urban environments. The proposed systems managed to follow lanes reliably in varying lighting conditions and were not disrupted by disturbances or shifts in trajectory. They were able to abide by traffic lights and speed limits and learned to execute different navigational commands at intersections.

Both systems managed to adapt its speed according to traffic, but their ability to respond to sudden changes varied. The CNN-LSTM were, by all indication, able to acquire some insight into the relationships between movement, distance, and change in the perceived size of objects. The regular CNN, interpreting each observation independently, was not able to learn these essential temporal dependencies. Hence, the results suggest that exploiting temporal information in subsequent images improves an end-to-end systems ability to drive reliably in an urban environment.

Even though the systems' performed several mistakes during testing, their achievements demonstrated great potential for using end-to-end systems to accomplish fully autonomous driving in urban environments.

# References

1. Bojarski, M., et al.: End to end learning for self-driving cars. CoRR abs/1604.07316 (2016). http://arxiv.org/abs/1604.07316
2. Codevilla, F., Müller, M., Dosovitskiy, A., López, A., Koltun, V.: End-to-end driving via conditional imitation learning. CoRR abs/1710.02410 (2017). http://arxiv.org/abs/1710.02410
3. Dosovitskiy, A., Ros, G., Codevilla, F., López, A., Koltun, V.: CARLA: an open urban driving simulator. CoRR abs/1711.03938 (2017). http://arxiv.org/abs/1711.03938
4. Eraqi, H.M., Moustafa, M.N., Honer, J.: End-to-end deep learning for steering autonomous vehicles considering temporal dependencies. CoRR abs/1710.03804 (2017). http://arxiv.org/abs/1710.03804
5. Haavaldsen, H., Aasbø, M.: Autonomous driving using a CNN: an example of end-to-end learning. https://youtu.be/Q37jTFZjK2s
6. Haavaldsen, H., Aasbø, M.: Autonomous driving using a CNN-LSTM: an example of end-to-end learning. https://youtu.be/ADzEHGmIDQQ
7. Hubschneider, C., Bauer, A., Weber, M., Zöllner, J.M.: Adding navigation to the equation: turning decisions for end-to-end vehicle control. In: 2017 IEEE 20th International Conference on Intelligent Transportation Systems (ITSC), pp. 1–8, October 2017. https://doi.org/10.1109/ITSC.2017.8317923
8. Kingma, D.P., Ba, J.: Adam: a method for stochastic optimization. In: 3rd International Conference on Learning Representations, ICLR 2015, Conference Track Proceedings, San Diego, CA, USA, 7–9 May 2015 (2015). http://arxiv.org/abs/1412.6980
9. Lecun, Y., Cosatto, E., Ben, J., Muller, U., Flepp, B.: Dave: autonomous off-road vehicle control using end-to-end learning. Technical report DARPA-IPTO Final Report, Courant Institute/CBLL (2004). http://www.cs.nyu.edu/~yann/research/dave/index.html
10. Pomerleau, D.A.: ALVINN: an autonomous land vehicle in a neural network. In: Advances in Neural Information Processing Systems 1, pp. 305–313. Morgan Kaufmann Publishers Inc., San Francisco (1989). http://dl.acm.org/citation.cfm?id=89851.89891

# Identifying Cross Country Skiing Techniques Using Power Meters in Ski Poles

Moa Johansson[✉], Marie Korneliusson, and Nickey Lizbat Lawrence

Chalmers University of Technology, Gothenburg, Sweden
moa.johansson@chalmers.se, {marieko,nickey}@student.chalmers.se

**Abstract.** Power meters are widely used for measuring training and racing effort in cycling, and the use of such sensors is now spreading also to other sports. Data collected from athletes' power meters are used to help coaches analyse and understand training load, racing efforts, technique etc. In this pilot project, we have collaborated with Skisens AB, a company producing handles for cross country ski poles equipped with power meters. We have conducted a pilot study on the use of machine learning techniques on sensor data from Skisens poles to identify which sub-technique a skier is using (double poling or gears 2–4 in skating). The dataset contain labelled time-series data from three individual skiers using four different sub-techniques recorded in varied locations and varied terrain. We evaluated three machine learning models based on neural networks, with best results obtained by a LSTM network (accuracy of 95% correctly classified strokes), when a subset of data from all three skiers was used for training. As expected, accuracy dropped to 78% when the model was trained on data from only two skiers and tested on the third.

## 1 Introduction

The development of a wide range of sensors and products such as GPS, heart-rate monitors, motion sensors and power sensors have made it possible to record a vast amount of data from athletes, providing a rich source of information to help coaches and athletes measure, analyse and understand training load, racing efforts and technique. Sports like cycling has lead the way among the endurance sports, as it its relatively easy to equip a bicycle with various sensors, for instance, to accurately measure the power in each pedal stroke. Given the relative ease at which large volumes of data can be recorded from sensors, we believe that machine learning has the potential to provide valuable tools for assisting data analysis in sports. In this pilot project, we have collaborated with Skisens AB, a spin-off company from Chalmers University of Technology that is developing a power meter for cross-country skiing, mounted inside the handle of the pole. Unlike cycling where all power comes from the legs via the pedals, in skiing the proportion of power measured in the poles depends on skiing technique. Broadly speaking, the skiing techniques are divided into classical style and freestyle, each regulated by rules in competition. Furthermore, the two styles can each be broken

© Springer Nature Switzerland AG 2019
K. Bach and M. Ruocco (Eds.): NAIS 2019, CCIS 1056, pp. 52–57, 2019.
https://doi.org/10.1007/978-3-030-35664-4_5

down into several sub-techniques. The most effective sub-technique will depend on the terrain, the snow conditions and the individual strengths of the skier. In order for an athlete and/or coach to accurately analyse the effort based on data recorded from a race it is therefore valuable to be able to get an automated classification of which sub-technique was used where during the race. This work focuses on free-style technique, however, the methods may be applied also to classical style.

A longer version of this paper is available as a technical report [5].

## 2  Related Work

There has been several previous works aiming at classifying cross-country skiing technique using a variety of sensors, following the initial experiments with wearable sensors by Marshland et al. [6]. Stöggl et al. used accelerometer data from a mobile phone attached to a belt around the chest of the skier and a Markov chain model to classify strokes [3,11]. Rindal et al. used wearable inertial measurement units (IMUs) attached to the skiers arms and chest, together with gyroscopes attached to the skiers arms [8]. Sakurai et al. also used data from several IMUs attached to the skis and poles to construct a decision tree classifier both for classical and skating techniques [9,10]. Recently, Jang et al. conducted a study using wearable gyroscope sensors to identify both classical and skating techniques and a deep machine learning model combining CNN and LSTM layers [4]. The main difference between our work and the above ski technique classifiers is that we do not use any dedicated wearable sensors for the task, but simply explore if we can identify technique using only the sensors already present in the Skisens pole for measuring power. Our sensor data only records the movements of the hands, and does not include any sensors on the body or on the skis, which would make the task easier.

## 3  The Dataset

The dataset consists of data from three individuals (male, experienced recreational skiers). The data was collected on roller skis on different days, in varied terrain and under varied conditions. There were both uphill and downhill sections as well as turns, with skiers using double poling plus three different skating styles, referred to as Gear 2, Gear 3 and Gear 4, following notation in [7][1]. For each gear there are a number of disjoint data segments, where each segment is a continuous time-series of data during which the skier only uses a specified style. The data collected is summarised in Table 1. Data was recorded at 50 Hz (50 samples per second), hence when we refer to time-steps, these are recorded 0.02 s apart. The raw data was pre-processed and longer segments divided into short segments, containing a single stroke each. The resulting dataset contains

---

[1] We note that the notation varies between different countries, these techniques are sometimes also referred to as V1, V2 and V2a. See [7] for a discussion.

1671 individual strokes, of which 252 strokes in Gear 2, 473 in Gear 3, 360 in Gear 4 and 585 strokes using double poling. Each single-stroke sample is 140 time-steps long, zero-padded when necessary.

**Table 1.** Description of the dataset columns used for machine learning. The coordinate system for the vectors of acceleration and angular velocity is relative to the pole with (a) First axis: pointing right (orthogonal to pole), (b) Second axis: pointing down (parallel to pole), and (c) Third axis: pointing forward (orthogonal to pole)

| No. | Data | Unit |
| --- | --- | --- |
| 1 | Time | second |
| 2 | Force in the left pole | Newton |
| 3 | Pole-ground angle of the left pole | degrees |
| 4–6 | Left angular velocity | rad/s |
| 7–9 | Left acceleration | $m/s^2$ |
| 10 | Force in the right pole | Newton |
| 11 | Pole-ground angle of the right pole | degree |
| 12–14 | Right angular velocity | rad/s |
| 15–17 | Right acceleration | $m/s^2$ |

We remark that the data recorded also included the GPS position, but we choose not to include this information as a feature. Different techniques are naturally used at distinct road segments, as some techniques are more natural to use e.g. in uphill terrain. If this was included, the models would end up basing their predictions primarily on GPS-position, ignoring the other features, which would lead to poor performance on unseen data recorded in a different location.

## 4  Machine Learning Models

We experimented with three different types of deep machine learning models for stroke classification: a long short term memory network (LSTM) [2], a bidirectional long short term memory network (BLSTM) [1], and a one dimensional convolutional neural network (CNN). The models were implemented in Python using the Keras/TensorFlow libraries[2]. The code is available online[3].

The LSTM model in our experiment combines an LSTM cell with two dense layers (see Fig. 1). The input of the LSTM model is a sequence of 140 time-steps, corresponding to one pole push. The number of neurons in each layer was chosen experimentally. The two dense layers can be interpreted as a weighted majority vote, weighing the importance of each time-step for giving a result of the most likely class for the entire pole push.

The BLSTM network has the same basic architecture as the LSTM network, but with 64 neurons in the first layer (chosen experimentally). While the LSTM

---

[2] https://www.tensorflow.org/guide/keras.
[3] https://github.com/moajohansson/ai-in-sports.

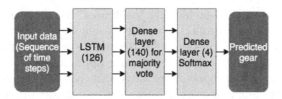

**Fig. 1.** Network architecture for the LSTM model, with an LSTM cell with two dense layer. The light blue boxes indicates layers in the network, and the number of neurons in each layer is stated inside the brackets in each layer. (Color figure online)

network passes information only in the forward direction, the BLSTM network passes information in both the forward and backward direction, thus using twice as many weights.

Our CNN model consists of two one-dimensional convolutional layers and two dense layers (see Fig. 2), as well as max-pooling and global max-pooling layers. The latter two layers are used for down-sampling, locally and globally. Number of neurons, filters, kernel- and pool size were decided experimentally.

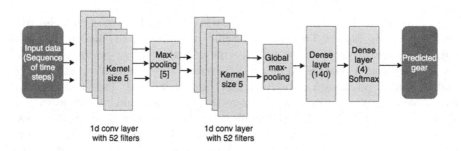

**Fig. 2.** The network architecture for the CNN model.

## 5   Experiments and Results

We conducted two experiments to assess classification accuracy. In Experiment 1, both the training set and unseen test set contain data from all three skiers. In Experiment 2, two skiers are used for training and the third for testing.

**Experiment 1:** We trained the models on a subset of the data containing samples from all three skiers, and evaluated on another, unseen, subset as test data. We suspect that the same person performs strokes in the same techniques in a relatively consistent manner, hence the strokes in the test set are likely to be quite similar to something from the training set. A motivation for this kind of experiment is envisaging an application using Skisens-sensors which is personalised to the owner, who initially "calibrates" the product by skiing using specified sub-techniques to collect personal training data.

Experiment 1 was performed for all three models described above, using five-fold cross-validation, with each fold containing approximately the same number of strokes and the same proportion of strokes in each sub-technique (folds 1–4 of 329 strokes, fold 5 of 355 strokes, from the total dataset of 1671 strokes).

The results are promising with both the LSTM and BLSTM models reaching an accuracy of 95% on average over the five folds. We note that the CNN model performed slightly worse than the other two, reaching an average accuracy of 90%, with higher variation over the different folds. We suspect that the CNN model suffered more than the LSTM-based models from the relatively small dataset. We note that the LSTM-based models also contains more trainable parameters than the CNN-model, so more experimentation is needed with different CNN architectures. Training took about 6–10 times longer for the LSTM and BLSTM models compared to the CNN model.

For the best-performing model (LSTM), we note that Gear 4 and double poling were the easiest to classify, while Gear 3 was the hardest. This was somewhat surprising, as the arm movements of Gear 4 and double poling are visually quite similar.

**Experiment 2:** Experiment 1 does not test the capability to generalise to a person not seen before. This was somewhat difficult to test, due to the small dataset. However, we did a second experiment with the best-performing model from Experiment 1 (the LSTM model) where we trained on data from two skiers, and evaluated on unseen data from the third individual. This was expected to be harder, as the model would have to generalise, and ideally learn how an "average" stroke in each sub-technique would be represented by the sensor data. As expected, performance dropped to 78%. We believe that this could be improved by training on a larger dataset with samples from many individuals, and performing a larger study is future work.

## 6    Discussion and Further Work

We have conducted a pilot study using data from sensors fitted to ski pole handles to predict which technique or gear the skier is using. This experiment aimed at classifying time-series for single strokes, as these are easy to identify from the power data recorded from the poles (near-zero readings indicating when the poles are in the air). We have not yet attempted the task of passing in continuous sequences of skiing strokes and identifying gear changes. This is an interesting problem, as some previous work, e.g. [8], report that mis-classifications of single strokes often happen near change points.

Most other works in cross-country skiing technique classification come from the sports science domain, and often include only a few individuals in the studies (e.g. 10 skiers in [8], four skiers in [4]). Furthermore, these studies often primarily focus on reaching high accuracy for these specific individuals (often elite athletes).

Experiments are often in the style of our Experiment 1, i.e. the training set and test set contain data from the same individuals. On this task, our LSTM model reached an accuracy of 95%, which is similar to other models from the literature [3, 8, 11]. In the setting of Experiment 2, with tests on unseen individuals, Jang et al. [4], reports an accuracy of between 87.2%–95.1%, compared to ours at 78%, but they had access to more data.

Our dataset, of merely 1671 strokes, is on the small side for deep learning, as seen in Experiment 2. We are however encouraged by the results in this study to gather a larger dataset and perform a larger evaluation. We would like a dataset containing both professional and recreational skiers to investigate whether one can train a model to generalise without taking small individual variations into account. This is particularly relevant from the perspective of Skisens, as they are interested in including technique classification together with their ski-pole sensors in for example a smart sports watch. Ideally, one would like to have a pre-trained model which does an acceptable job out of the box, and possibly then adapts to the individual user, without having to be trained from scratch.

# References

1. Graves, A., Schmidhuber, J.: Framewise phoneme classification with bidirectional LSTM and other neural network architectures. Neural Netw. **18**, 602–610 (2005)
2. Hochreiter, S., Schmidhuber, J.: Long short-term memory. Neural Comput. **9**, 1735–1780 (1997)
3. Hols, A., Jonasson, A.: Classification of movement patterns in skiing. In: Frontiers in Artificial Intelligence and Applications: Twelfth Scandinavian Conference on Artificial Intelligence, vol. 257 (2013)
4. Jang, J., et al.: A unified deep-learning model for classifying the cross-country skiing techniques using wearable gyroscope sensors. Sensors **18**(11), 3819 (2018)
5. Johansson, M., Korneliusson, M., Lizbat Lawrence, N.: Identifying cross country skiing techniques using power meters in skipoles. arxiv.org/abs/1904.10359 (2019)
6. Marshland, F., Lyons, K., Anson, J., Waddington, G., Macintosh, C., Chapman, D.: Identification of cross-country skiing movement patterns using micro-sensors. Sensors **12**(4), 5047–5066 (2012)
7. Nilsson, J., Tveit, P., Eikrehagen, O.: Effects of speed on temporal patterns in classical style and freestyle cross-country skiing. Sports Biomech. **3**(1), 85–107 (2004)
8. Rindal, O., Seeberg, T., Tjønnås, J., Haugnes, P., Sandbakk, Ø.: Automatic classification of sub-techniques in classical cross-country skiing using a machine learning algorithm on micro-sensor data. Sensors **18**(2), 75 (2017)
9. Sakurai, Y., Zenya, F., Ishige, Y.: Automated identification and evaluation of sub-techniques in classical-style roller skiing. J. Sports Sci. Med. **13**, 651–657 (2014)
10. Sakurai, Y., Zenya, F., Ishige, Y.: Automatic identification of subtechniques in skating-style roller skiing using inertial sensors. Sensors **16**, 473 (2016)
11. Stöggl, T., et al.: Automatic classification of the sub-techniques (gears) used in cross-country ski skating employing a mobile phone. Sensors **14**, 20589–20601 (2014)

# Experiences from Real-World Evolution with DyRET: Dynamic Robot for Embodied Testing

Tønnes F. Nygaard[1(✉)], Jørgen Nordmoen[1], Kai Olav Ellefsen[1],
Charles P. Martin[1,2], Jim Tørresen[1,2], and Kyrre Glette[1,2]

[1] Department of Informatics, University of Oslo, Oslo, Norway
tonnesfn@ifi.uio.no
[2] RITMO Center of Excellence, University of Oslo, Oslo, Norway

**Abstract.** Creating robust robot platforms that function in the real world is a difficult task. Adding the requirement that the platform should be capable of learning, from nothing, ways to generate its own movement makes the task even harder. Evolutionary Robotics is a promising field that combines the creativity of evolutionary optimization with the real-world focus of robotics to bring about unexpected control mechanisms in addition to whole new robot designs. Constructing a platform that is capable of these feats is difficult, and it is important to share experiences and lessons learned so that designers of future robot platforms can benefit. In this paper, we introduce our robotics platform and detail our experiences with real-world evolution. We present thoughts on initial design considerations and key insights we have learned from extensive experimentation. We hope to inspire new platform development and hopefully reduce the threshold of doing real-world legged robot evolution.

**Keywords:** Evolutionary robotics · Real-world evolution · Lessons learned

## 1 Introduction

Robots are used in more and more complex environments, and are expected to be able to adapt themselves to changes and unknown situations. The easiest and quickest way to adapt is to change the control system of the robot, but for increasingly complex environments one should also change the body of the robot—its morphology—to better fit the task at hand [1]. To achieve this vision, researchers need access to flexible robot platforms that can be adapted to new environments and tasks. For many projects this limits choices to simulated experiments on virtual robots that are never tested in the real world.

This work is partially supported by The Research Council of Norway under grant agreement 240862 and through its Centers of Excellence scheme, project number 262762. Simulations with DyRET were performed on resources provided by UNINETT Sigma2 - the National Infrastructure for High Performance Computing and Data Storage in Norway.

K. Bach and M. Ruocco (Eds.): NAIS 2019, CCIS 1056, pp. 58–68, 2019.
https://doi.org/10.1007/978-3-030-35664-4_6

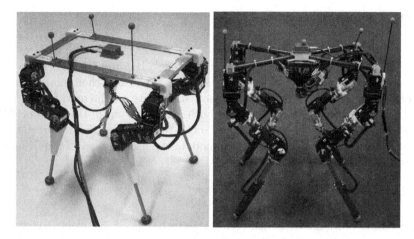

**Fig. 1.** Initial version of DyRET (left) without self-modifying legs. Latest version of DyRET (right) with fully extended legs.

*Evolutionary Robotics* takes inspiration from natural evolution, with concepts such as hereditary traits and genome mutation, and applies these principles to robotics. This combination has shown incredible creativity, not only creating novel robot controllers but, going as far as creating whole new robot bodies. However, this creativity is usually constrained to the software realm due to the ease of simulating these new creations and the difficulty in performing the same number of experiments in the real world. In contrast to the majority of work in Evolutionary Robotics, Eiben argues for real-world experiments in his "Grand Challenges for Evolutionary Robotics" [2]. This requires robust hardware platforms that are capable of repeated experiments. At the same time, these platforms must be flexible to manage unforeseen demands.

An emerging concept within evolutionary robotics is the theory of *Embodied Cognition*. This theory suggests that reasoning and cognition cannot be fully understood if studied in simple computer models alone. The mind, body, environment, and the interaction between these all contribute as cognitive resources [3]. Taking advantage of these concepts could lead to improved adaptivity, robustness, and versatility [4], however, executing these concepts on real-world robots puts additional requirements on the hardware and raises several challenges when compared to learning just control [5].

In this paper, we will present related work before introducing our robot platform with self-adaptive morphology, seen in Fig. 1. The main section of the paper will describe the challenges we have faced when designing the robot, and the lessons learned from real-world evolution and experimentation. By summarizing our experiences we can report on key insights which can hopefully lead to better robotics platforms in the future.

## 2   Background

Robots are becoming a more widely used tool in many industries, and are used for advanced tasks and in complex environments. Historically wheeled robots have been used extensively in industrial settings because of their simplicity and ease of deployment [6]. However, we are now starting to see the need for robots to operate in more complex environments, both inside and out in the real world [7]. Using legs instead of wheels allows the robot to traverse difficult terrains and environments, making the robot accommodate the user instead of requiring the user to adapt to the robot.

### 2.1   Evolutionary Robotics

The field of Evolutionary Robotics (ER) uses techniques from evolutionary computation to optimize both a robot's control and body [8]. Many different legged robots have been used in ER research. Some use off-the-shelf standard robots not specifically designed for ER research, like Sony's Aibo [9], while others use robots specifically built for the purpose, like the Aracna [10].

Most earlier work in ER only optimize the control system of the robot [2]. This can allow the robot to adapt to the environment it is operating in [11], or to changes to the robot itself [12]. However, only changing the control has its limitations, and earlier work has shown that changing the morphology yields results that could not be achieved by changing control alone [13]. Furthermore, most work is done on virtual robots in simplified physics simulations, and not on actual physical robots [14]. This allows for simple parallelization and noise-free evaluations, but the inaccuracies in the simulator or models used often lead to big discrepancies in the performance of the virtual robot and its real world counterpart [15]. In simple cases these discrepancies can lead to differing performance when transferring from simulation to the real world and can in the worst cases lead the optimization algorithm to focus on behaviors that are not possible to perform at all in the real world. Within the field of ER this challenge is known as *the reality gap* and is one of the biggest hurdles facing robotics researchers currently [16]. There are many techniques to reduce the reality gap [17], but even with recent strides [18], this is becoming more and more challenging, as both the robots themselves, the environment they operate in, and the tasks they are solving become more complex and harder to model.

### 2.2   Embodied Cognition

The theory of Embodied Cognition originally came from psychology, but is making its way into many sub-fields of robotics, including swarm robotics and modular robotics [19]. The original theory states that the brain is not the only cognitive resource a human has, and that the body, the environment, and the interactions between these can also serve as cognitive resources [3]. There are several examples where this has been used successfully in robotics [20]. An important aspect of this approach, is that a large part of the cognition, or problem solving ability of a robot, can be placed in the robot body, its environment, and the interactions these form with each other and the robot controller. Therefore, inaccurate models of either environment or body can make it impossible to accurately exhibit Embodied Cognition on anything but the physical robot in the real world [2].

## 3   The 'DyRET' Robot

Our robot, DyRET (Dynamic Robot for Embodied Testing), was developed to be a platform for experiments on self-adaptive morphologies and embodied cognition [21], shown in Fig. 2. It is a fully certified open source hardware project, and documentation, code and design files are freely available online [22]. Since it is intended for use with machine learning techniques it is designed to be robust, so that is can withstand falls from unstable gaits [23]. It can actively reconfigure its morphology by changing the lengths of its femurs and tibias. Shorter leg length increases the force at the end of the leg, given constant torque from the servo. The self-changing morphology therefore allows the robot to change the trade-off between movement speed and force surplus continuously, and can serve as a gearing of the motor [24].

**Fig. 2.** Top and left views of our reconfigurable robotic platform, and examples of the legs at two different lengths.

The robot is built using *Commercial-off-the-shelf* (COTS) components where possible, and all custom parts can be made with consumer grade 3D printers. We also use composite tubing for structural integrity. Selected parts have an alternative design in aluminium for more demanding requirements, and have been milled. Dynamixel servos are used in all rotational joints, which feature on-board PID controllers for accurate position control. The servos are connected to a common bus that interfaces to a computer over USB. The length of each leg segment is controlled by a custom linear actuator, driven by a standard DC motor. The main mechanism consists of a lead screw that moves carriages along two rails using a chain, all COTS components. An encoder gives the position of each actuator, and a simple positional controller is run on an Arduino Mega board with a custom interface shield. The robot features an XSense MTi-30 Attitude and Heading Reference System that measures linear acceleration, rotational velocity and absolute orientation. The robot has reflective markers that is used with motion capture equipment to get the absolute position of the robot. It also features directional force sensors mounted on each foot which can be used to detect when the feet touch the ground.

## 4    Experiences and Challenges

In this section, we present some key lessons we have learned when working with DyRET. We have tried to summarize the lessons, followed by more detailed explanations.

---

**Initial design considerations**

Robustness and maintainability are more important than ease of building. Using *rapid prototyping* and *design for manufacturability* principles, along with exploiting *Commercial-Off-The-Shelf* components are crucial in achieving an effective design process of a legged robot.

---

Legged robots are very complex systems, and anticipating all demands and challenges early in the design process is impossible. Techniques from *rapid prototyping* allowed us to quickly get physical prototypes of the robot, which allowed us to see and fix challenges that would be difficult to find without having physical proof-of-concept models of the system available. An important part of this, is to use already existing Commercial-Off-The-Shelf (COTS) components where available. This allows us to capitalize on the work of others, and also makes it easier for others to build or utilize lessons learned from our designs. *Design for manufacturability* is another important concept, and promotes adapting the design to manufacturing considerations during the initial design process, where they can be solved much more easily than during operation. As an example of this we have included the designs in Fig. 3 which illustrates how the manufacturing methods should help inform the design of the individual parts. Making a robot that is easy and cheap to build can be important, but our experience is that maintainability is even more important, especially when using machine learning that puts considerable strains on the physical robot.

**Fig. 3.** The two parts on the left are designed for two different 3D printers while the part on the right is designed for milling. This is an example of designing for manufacturability where parts are designed for the same purpose, but optimized for different manufacturing methods.

---

**Repairs and mechanical failures**

A good strategy for redesign is important to balance quick spot repairs and laborious systematic analyses of failures. Increasing the strength of individual parts that break is often not an effective way to do iterative design.

---

Designing parts for legged robots is always a trade-off between strength and weight, and mechanical failures during prototyping is guaranteed. Strengthening the part that broke can be a quick fix, but our experience is that this often results in the problem being transferred to other parts of the robot. Both high persistent forces and sudden shock travel through the mechanical design, and lead to failures in the next weakest link of the chain. Reducing stress concentrations locally in a particular part can sometimes be successful in allowing the robot to withstand a similar situation again, however, excessive force can often lead to cascading failures throughout the system. An example of this can be seen in Fig. 4, where a strengthening of a part that broke lead to the next part in the chain breaking instead. Having a clear strategy for when and what to do when mechanical failures happen is important, and early on deciding on a balance between quick spot repairs and laborious systematic analyses of failures. Once an experiment is underway, replacing parts with similar parts might be the only option without skewing the results, so extra efforts on failure identification during the prototyping phase might be worth the effort. Larger cracks in the material are often easy to identify, but deflection during operation, small fractures, or material creep can be harder to detect.

**Fig. 4.** An example showing a cascading mechanical failure, where an initial strengthening of a broken part (left, and circled blue on the right) leads to a failure in the next part in the chain (red circle) (Color figure online).

---

**Controller complexity**

Low controller complexity puts less strain on the robot by testing solutions that are safer and more conservative, and is quicker to optimize. High complexity controllers can give better results by having higher freedom, but will necessarily test solutions that are incautious. This complexity trade-off is often not considered when doing simulation-only experiments, but can be imperative when working on physical robots.

---

Learning legged locomotion is a difficult challenge. To optimize the walking pattern, the gait, the movement of the legs is parameterized through a gait controller. Much a priori knowledge can be embedded into the controller, resulting in few parameters that are easy to optimize. Less prior knowledge requires more of the optimization algorithm, resulting in an increased number of evaluations. The more knowledge that is embedded, the less room there is for a varied range of behaviors, which might be needed to adapt to new or changing tasks, environments or the robot itself [25]. Finding the right complexity balance can be very challenging, especially in real-world learning where the number of evaluations are limited. We have successfully used a gait controller with dynamic complexity [26], which can be seen in Fig. 5. Another option is using different controllers for different environments or tasks [27], for instance a complex controller when optimizing the gait in a simulator with cheap evaluations, and a less complex controller in the real world.

---

**Starting in the real world**

Using a virtual robot can be a quick way to get started learning locomotion. It is, however, more difficult to transition from abstract simulated robots to the real world, compared to going from a physical system to simulation.

---

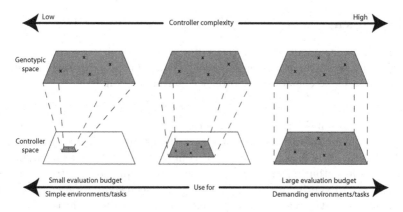

**Fig. 5.** Diagram of a controller with adaptable gait complexity. Here, a dynamic genotype-phenotype mapping allows a single parameter to control the complexity of generated gaits in-turn affording the experimenter the ability to trade-off optimization demands with task/environment difficulty [26].

Evaluating solutions on a physical robot system can take seconds to several minutes, depending on gait complexity and experiment design. Evaluating in physics simulations or with simplified models, often done in software, can give a speedup of several orders of magnitude. This often makes simulation a flexible and easy starting point. However, our experience with DyRET indicates that going from a real-world robot to simulation can yield more realistic simulation results which in turn translates to more sensible real-world gaits after software optimization. Not basing a virtual robot on a physical prototype makes it easier to make choices resulting in solutions that turn out to be infeasible in the real world [14], illustrated in Fig. 6.

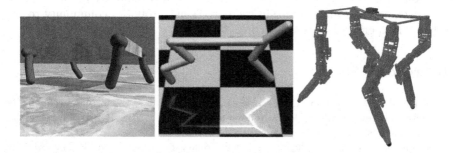

**Fig. 6.** Comparison of different legged robots in simulation, with DyRET on the right. Since DyRET was first designed in hardware and then transferred to simulation it is known that it would function in the real world after simulation. In contrast, the first two simulated robots, on the left, were designed without these constraints making it difficult to predict how algorithms applied to these will function on real-world counterparts.

> **Experiment design**
>
> Both the environment and the robot itself are dynamic, and changes will happen during operation. This can lead to biases in the experiment results, which have to be controlled by proper experiment design.

One of the key insights we have experienced after real-world experiments on DyRET is how components change characteristics during the course of experiments. Because of this gradual change, it is important to store as much information as possible so that automatic procedures can be applied to detect differences during and after experiments. A big difference between simulation and real-world experiments is that a real-world experiment can never be perfectly replicated. The change in characteristics should also guide the experiment design in the real world. Because components are expected to change, it is important to evenly test different solutions so as to not bias the experiment towards a specific one [28, Chapter 11]. A specific example is the reduction in performance of our joints as the motors heat up. If the solutions are always tested in the same order, this might affect the results, and give spurious effects that can result in noise or skew in the collected data.

## 5   Conclusion

In this paper we have presented lessons learned through extensive experimentation on the DyRET platform. This includes both initial design considerations, and challenges such as the trade-off between simulated experiments and real world evolution. Having a mechanically self-modifying quadruped robot is rare among platforms used in evolutionary robotics research. This gives us a unique insight into evolution of control and morphology in the real world. By sharing knowledge usually not found in experiment-based publications, we hope to encourage more researchers within the evolutionary robotics community to try real-world experiments.

## References

1. Nygaard, T.F., Martin, C.P., Torresen, J., Glette, K.: Exploring mechanically self-reconfiguring robots for autonomous design. In: 2018 ICRA Workshop on Autonomous Robot Design (2018)
2. Eiben, A.E.: Grand challenges for evolutionary robotics. Front. Robot. AI **1**, 4 (2014)
3. Wilson, A., Golonka, S.: Embodied cognition is not what you think it is. Front. Psychol. **4**, 58 (2013)
4. Nordmoen, J., Nygaard, T.F., Ellefsen, K.O., Glette, K.: Evolved embodied phase coordination enables robust quadruped robot locomotion. In: Proceedings of the Genetic and Evolutionary Computation Conference. ACM (2019)

5. Nygaard, T.F., Samuelsen, E., Glette, K.: Overcoming initial convergence in multi-objective evolution of robot control and morphology using a two-phase approach. In: Squillero, G., Sim, K. (eds.) EvoApplications 2017. LNCS, vol. 10199, pp. 825–836. Springer, Cham (2017). https://doi.org/10.1007/978-3-319-55849-3_53

6. Silva, M.F., Tenreiro Machado, J.: A historical perspective of legged robots. J. Vib. Control 13(9–10), 1447–1486 (2007)

7. Bares, J.E., Whittaker, W.L.: Configuration of autonomous walkers for extreme terrain. Int. J. Robot. Res. 12(6), 535–559 (1993)

8. Doncieux, S., Bredeche, N., Mouret, J.-B., Eiben, A.E.G.: Evolutionary robotics: what, why, and where to. Front. Robot. AI 2, 4 (2015)

9. Hornby, G.S., Takamura, S., Yokono, J., Hanagata, O., Yamamoto, T., Fujita, M.: Evolving robust gaits with AIBO. In: IEEE International Conference on Robotics and Automation, vol. 3, pp. 3040–3045. IEEE (2000)

10. Lohmann, S., Yosinski, J., Gold, E., Clune, J., Blum, J., Lipson, H.: Aracna: an open-source quadruped platform for evolutionary robotics. In: Artificial Life Conference Proceedings 12, pp. 387–392. MIT Press (2012)

11. Haasdijk, E., Bredeche, N., Eiben, A.E.: Combining environment-driven adaptation and task-driven optimisation in evolutionary robotics. Plos one 9(6), 1–14 (2014)

12. Koos, S., Cully, A., Mouret, J.-B.: Fast damage recovery in robotics with the t-resilience algorithm. Int. J. Robot. Res. 32(14), 1700–1723 (2013)

13. Picardi, G., Hauser, H., Laschi, C., Calisti, M.: Morphologically induced stability on an underwater legged robot with a deformable body. Int. J. Robot. Res. (2019) https://doi.org/10.1177/0278364919840426

14. Mouret, J.-B., Chatzilygeroudis, K.: 20 years of reality gap: a few thoughts about simulators in evolutionary robotics. In: Proceedings of the Genetic and Evolutionary Computation Conference Companion, pp. 1121–1124. ACM (2017)

15. Jakobi, N., Husbands, P., Harvey, I.: Noise and the reality gap: the use of simulation in evolutionary robotics. In: Morán, F., Moreno, A., Merelo, J.J., Chacón, P. (eds.) ECAL 1995. LNCS, vol. 929, pp. 704–720. Springer, Heidelberg (1995). https://doi.org/10.1007/3-540-59496-5_337

16. Silva, F., Duarte, M., Correia, L., Oliveira, S.M., Christensen, A.L.: Open issues in evolutionary robotics. Evol. Comput. 24(2), 205–236 (2016)

17. Koos, S., Mouret, J.-B., Doncieux, S.: The transferability approach: crossing the reality gap in evolutionary robotics. IEEE Trans. Evol. Comput. 17, 122–145 (2013)

18. Tobin, J., Fong, R., Ray, A., Schneider, J., Zaremba, W., Abbeel, P.: Domain randomization for transferring deep neural networks from simulation to the real world. In: 2017 IEEE/RSJ International Conference on Intelligent Robots and Systems (IROS), pp. 23–30. IEEE (2017)

19. Pfeifer, R., Gómez, G.: Morphological computation–connecting brain, body, and environment. In: Sendhoff, B., Körner, E., Sporns, O., Ritter, H., Doya, K. (eds.) Creating Brain-Like Intelligence. LNCS (LNAI), vol. 5436, pp. 66–83. Springer, Heidelberg (2009). https://doi.org/10.1007/978-3-642-00616-6_5

20. Hoffman, G.: Embodied cognition for autonomous interactive robots. Top. Cogn. Sci. 4(4), 759–772 (2012)

21. Nygaard, T.F., Martin, C.P., Torresen, J., Glette, K.: Self-modifying morphology experiments with DyRET: dynamic robot for embodied testing. In: 2019 IEEE International Conference on Robotics and Automation (ICRA) (2019)

22. Nygaard, T.F., Nordmoen, J.: DyRET software repository (2019). https://github.com/dyret-robot/dyret_documentation

23. Nygaard, T.F., Torresen, J., Glette, K.: Multi-objective evolution of fast and stable gaits on a physical quadruped robotic platform. In: IEEE Symposium Series on Computational Intelligence (SSCI), pp. 1–8 (2016)
24. Nygaard, T.F., Martin, C.P., Samuelsen, E., Torresen, J., Glette, K.: Real-world evolution adapts robot morphology and control to hardware limitations. In: Proceedings of the Genetic and Evolutionary Computation Conference. ACM (2018)
25. Nordmoen, J., Ellefsen, K.O., Glette, K.: Combining MAP-elites and incremental evolution to generate gaits for a mammalian quadruped robot. In: Sim, K., Kaufmann, P. (eds.) EvoApplications 2018. LNCS, vol. 10784, pp. 719–733. Springer, Cham (2018). https://doi.org/10.1007/978-3-319-77538-8_48
26. Nygaard, T.F., Martin, C.P., Torresen, J., Glette, K.: Evolving robots on easy mode: towards a variable complexity controller for quadrupeds. In: Kaufmann, P., Castillo, P.A. (eds.) EvoApplications 2019. LNCS, vol. 11454, pp. 616–632. Springer, Cham (2019). https://doi.org/10.1007/978-3-030-16692-2_41
27. Nordmoen, J., Samuelsen, E., Ellefsen, K.O., Glette, K.: Dynamic mutation in MAP-elites for robotic repertoire generation. In: Artificial Life Conference Proceedings, pp. 598–605. MIT Press (2018)
28. Ryan, T.P., Morgan, J.: Modern experimental design. J. Stat. Theory Pract. 1(3–4), 501–506 (2007)

# Effectiveness of Neural Networks for Research on Novel Thermoelectric Materials. A Proof of Concept

Filippo Remonato[1(✉)], Ole M. Løvvik[2], and Espen Flage-Larsen[2]

[1] Department of Applied Mathematics and Cybernetics,
SINTEF Digital, Oslo, Norway
`filippo.remonato@sintef.no`
[2] Department of Materials Physics, SINTEF Industri, Oslo, Norway
{`olemartin.lovvik,espen.flage-larsen`}`@sintef.no`

**Abstract.** This paper describes the application of neural network approaches to the discovery of new materials exhibiting thermoelectric properties. Thermoelectricity is the ability of a material to convert energy from heat to electricity. At present, only few materials are known to have this property to a degree which is interesting for use in industrial applications like, for example, large-scale energy harvesting [3,8]. We employ a standard neural network architecture with supervised learning on a training dataset representing materials and later predict the properties on a disjoint test set. At this proof of concept stage, both sets are synthetically generated with plausible values of the features. A substantial increase in performance is seen when utilising available physical knowledge in the machine learning model. The results show that this approach is feasible and ready for future tests with experimental laboratory data.

**Keywords:** Neural networks · Thermoelectric materials · Physics-oriented machine learning

## 1 Introduction

About 70% of the energy globally produced is released in the atmosphere as heat [2]. Given the predicted increase in energy demands, coupled with the pressure on our planet's resources and climate, it is clear we cannot afford to lose such, and it is therefore important to be able to recover the produced heat and use it in further processes. The most common way to recover waste heat is for heating buildings or smaller environments like a car. This produces already good results: An average fossil-fuel power plant is able to turn into electricity only about 30% of the energy contained in the fuel, but when the excess heat is recovered, the total efficiency rises to 60–80% [1]. However, heat is sub-optimal compared to other energy sources: It is difficult to transport, it is easily lost, and in general our technology to exploit heat is not particularly advanced. The reason why waste heat is mostly reused simply in its raw form is that heat has high entropy, it is difficult to transform it back into more valuable energy types. Thermoelectric

© Springer Nature Switzerland AG 2019
K. Bach and M. Ruocco (Eds.): NAIS 2019, CCIS 1056, pp. 69–77, 2019.
https://doi.org/10.1007/978-3-030-35664-4_7

materials accomplish just that: They are capable of generating an electrical current from a temperature difference, and are therefore highly valuable ingredients in heat recovery processes and development of new technologies.

This property of converting heat to electricity has sparked wide attention in several research communities and application areas [4, 6, 9]. Enabling the recovery and use of what was previously almost lost thermal energy, they are seen as an important step toward more sustainable, efficient, and circular industrial processes. Despite numerous ongoing researches, the amount of available data on thermoelectric materials is unfortunately still somewhat limited; this because most current state of the art techniques for theoretical material analysis make use of the density functional theory (DFT) [5], which is computationally relatively expensive [7]. In principle, DFT allows us to study in detail and precisely a variety of physical properties of a crystalline material, including whether the material in question presents good thermoelectric properties or not, but doing this for every possible material is clearly not yet feasible.

One quantity indicating how "thermoelectric" a material is, is the so called *figure of merit*, $ZT$, given by the formula:

$$ZT = \frac{T\sigma\alpha^2}{\kappa_E + \kappa_L},\tag{1}$$

Where $T$ is the temperature, $\sigma$ is the electrical conductivity, $\alpha$ is the Seebeck coefficient, $\kappa_E$ is the electronic part of the thermal conductivity, and $\kappa_L$ is the phonon part (lattice vibrations) of the thermal conductivity. A brief description of these and other physical quantities is given below in Sect. 2.1.

Machine learning (ML) is a collection of techniques, and the study of such techniques, to produce algorithms capable of inferring the solution to a given problem by analysing sets of (related) data. Machine learning algorithms have the distinctive property of being able to extrapolate from the provided data the often very complex underlying patterns linking input to output, in a "cause and effect" fashion. In this work we focus on using such techniques to predict the $ZT$ value given some physical descriptors of the materials.

We see this as a step toward a practical methodology where ML can be used to scan large parts of the input domain, i.e. the different materials compositions, in order to search for candidate thermoelectric materials. This will allow a laboratory to focus their research and computational efforts to few selected promising materials, thus accelerating the development of new technologies.

## 2   Methodology

The problem is handled with a classical regression/supervised learning approach: We first train our chosen neural network (NN) architecture using pairs $(x_i, ZT_i)$, where $x_i$ is a database entry vector collecting a material's information and $ZT_i$ is its associated $ZT$ value. Then we perform predictions on a test set containing datapoints which have not been used before.

## 2.1 The Database

The dataset we employed consisted of roughly 250000 synthetically-generated datapoints. The descriptors (features) included in the dataset are:

- *num bands*: The number of electronic bands included in the simulation, gives an idea of the complexity of the band structure around the chemical potential;
- *effmass arithmetic*: The effective mass of the charge carriers using the arithmetic mean, in units of the bare electron mass;
- *effmass geometric*: The effective mass of the charge carriers using the geometric mean, in units of the bare electron mass;
- *shift arithmetic*: The average energy shift from zero (location of the chemical potential on the energy scale where 0 eV is the energy reference), of all the electronic bands using the arithmetic mean, units of eV;
- *shift min*: The minimum energy shift (see definition of shift arithmetic);
- *shift max*: The maximum energy shift (see definition of shift arithmetic);
- *T*: The temperature in Kelvin;
- *chempot*: The chemical potential in eV;
- *n*: The free carrier concentration in $10^{21}$ cm$^{-3}$;
- *sigma*: The electrical conductivity, $\sigma$, in S/m;
- *seebeck*: The Seebeck coefficient, $\alpha$, in V/$\mu$K;
- *kappae*: The electronic part of the thermal conductivity carried by the electrons, $\kappa_E$, in units of W/(m · K);
- *ZT_01*: The value of $ZT$ when $\kappa_L = 0.1$ W/(m · K);
- *ZT_1*: The value of $ZT$ when $\kappa_L = 1$ W/(m · K);
- *ZT_10*: The value of $ZT$ when $\kappa_L = 10$ W/(m · K);

The descriptors' values were chosen in a plausible range, so that the tests, while not being connected to any application, could still be instructive regarding the feasibility and performance of this approach when enough real-world data is available. For a similar study performed on a smaller but real-world dataset, we reference the interested reader to [10]. The full dataset of 250000 samples has been randomly shuffled and split in a train set (0.6 fraction), validation set (0.2 fraction), and test set (0.2 fraction).

## 2.2 Features Selection

Not all of the descriptors listed above have been used in our ML model. To choose which descriptors to use as training features we employed a simple correlation analysis, selecting those that displayed high correlation with the target output and discarding those that are highly correlated with each other. The logic behind the former criteria is obvious: In order to exploit the approximating power of neural networks, the features used as input have to be meaningfully related to the target output. The reason for the latter criteria is that one wants to avoid over-representing some characteristics of the data. For example, it's clear that the descriptors effmass arithmetic and effmass geometric both represent the same information just in two different ways, therefore only one should be included in the training data.

We note that, since the dataset has been synthetically generated, one could think a correlation analysis approach is not necessary. However, we thought it meaningful to treat the dataset like if it contained unknown real-world data, and therefore applied the same strategies we would have applied in that case.

With the above in consideration, the descriptors that were selected as training features are: *num bands, effmass geometric, shift arithmetic, shift max, chempot,* and $n$. Note, in particular, that we did not select the values of $\sigma$, $\alpha$, and $\kappa_E$ as features since those quantities are the ones that are computed with the expensive DFT and the whole reason to use a NN to predict $ZT$ values is to avoid that step. Indeed, if the values of $\sigma$, $\alpha$, and $\kappa_E$ were available, one should employ the formula in (1) directly.

## 2.3   Neural Network Architecture

Since the purpose of this investigation was to check the feasibility of the approach, we didn't delve too much in fine-tuning the network's parameters and instead wanted to test how an almost out-of-the-box approach performed. For this reason we employed a very standard NN consisting of the input layer for the features, three hidden layers with 100 neurons each with Re-LU activation function, and output nodes, so that the results contained in this work form a baseline for further research and comparison. All layers are fully connected. Both the amount of neurons and number of hidden layers have been decided a priori, before doing any tests, and no regularisation, dropout, or other fine tuned features have been used, so that the results obtained here constitute indeed a lower bound for the quality and accuracy one can expect from this approach. The only tuning we performed was to prevent strongly overfitting the train data. This, staying true to the philosophy of keeping the network's parameters at a minimum, was achieved with early stopping based on the error on the validation set. The model has been constructed in Keras and trained using the Adams optimizer with default parameters values. As loss function we employed the standard mean square error between predictions and target values.

We tried two different choices of activation function for the output layer: In Test 1 no special function was employed, so that the last layer produced a simple linear output. Moreover, since the maximum values of the three $ZT$s differed at most by one order of magnitude, we did not normalise the target values. In Test 2, on the other hand, we wanted to use the physical knowledge at our disposal, namely that $ZT$ values are positive, to increase the performance of the NN approximation, and therefore enforced output values to be positive through the application of a sigmoid activation function on the last layer. Since the range of the sigmoid is $(0, 1)$, this also naturally called for the normalisation of the target values.

The two simple changes above considerably improved the performance of the model, as shown in the results below.

## 3   Results

### 3.1   Test 1

Our first test was conducted with a neural network consisting of an input layer with 6 input nodes, three hidden layers of 100 neurons each with Re-Lu activation function, and a *linear activation* output layer with 3 nodes, one for each value of $ZT$. The output data has not been normalised.

Figure 1a shows the training history, i.e. the loss function value, for both the train and validation set over the 400 training epochs.

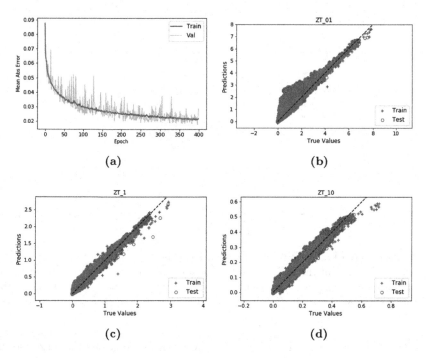

**Fig. 1. Test 1. (a)** The error function on the train and validation set during the training epochs. **(b)** The predictions for $ZT_{0.1}$ on train and test set. **(c)** The predictions for $ZT_1$ on train and test set. **(d)** The predictions for $ZT_{10}$ on train and test set. The black dashed line is the bisector of the first quadrant.

Probably thanks to the fact that our dataset is synthetically generated, and therefore we have ample quantity of data and no skewed classes, no appreciable overfitting in the model is observed. The decision to early-stop training at 400 epochs was taken because that is the point at which the validation error reaches a plateau. We also note that although the general trend of the $ZT$ values is correctly identified, the accuracy of the prediction is somewhat coarse. This becomes even more apparent when plotting the same data as in Figs. 1b–1d on a logarithmic scale, to better see the differences in orders of magnitude. Figure 2 shows that the network fails for small values, with the predictions being several orders of magnitude off.

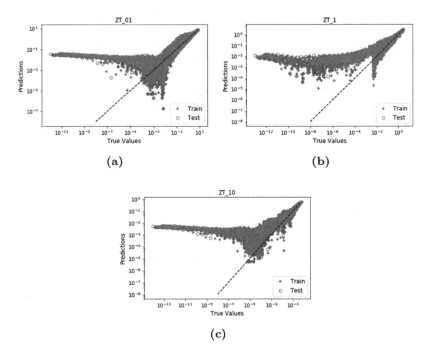

**Fig. 2. Test 1. (a)** Logarithmic plot of the predictions for $ZT_{0.1}$ on train and test set. **(b)** Logarithmic plot of the predictions for $ZT_1$ on train and test set. **(c)** Logarithmic plot of the predictions for $ZT_{10}$ on train and test set. The black dashed line is the bisector of the first quadrant.

It has to be remarked that the accuracy in the predictions for large values of $ZT$, which is the area of interest, is acceptable, but the strange behaviour exemplified in Fig. 2 made us wonder whether we could improve the performance by adding just a little of physical knowledge to the model; this led us to Test 2.

### 3.2    Test 2

In the second test we incorporated some physical knowledge into the model. In particular we enforced the output of only positive values by applying a sigmoid activation function to the last layer in place of the normal linear activation. Since the sigmoid range is in $(0, 1)$, the target output has also been normalised before training. Figure 3 shows the results in this case.

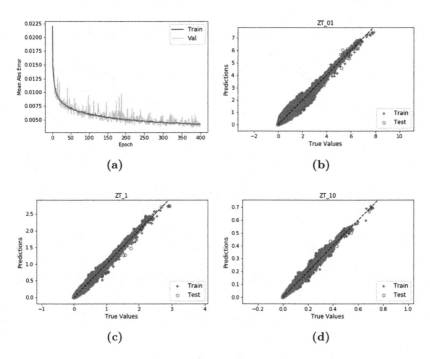

**Fig. 3. Test 2. (a)** The error function on the train and validation set during the training epochs. (b) The predictions for $ZT_{0.1}$ on train and test set. (c) The predictions for $ZT_1$ on train and test set. (d) The predictions for $ZT_{10}$ on train and test set. The black dashed line is the bisector of the first quadrant.

As before, no appreciable overfitting is found, but the accuracy of the predictions is sensibly improved as the bands around the diagonal line are narrower. This is visible also from the error recorded in the training history, Fig. 3a, which after 400 epochs is about four times lower than that in Test 1.

The change in behaviour of the model transpires clearly also in the logarithmic plots for the predictions, displayed in Fig. 4. Now the network predicts accurately across the entire range of values, with errors well within acceptable range.

The introduction of the sigmoid function in the last layer, forcing the NN to learn only positive values, has thus substantially improved the overall performance of the ML model.

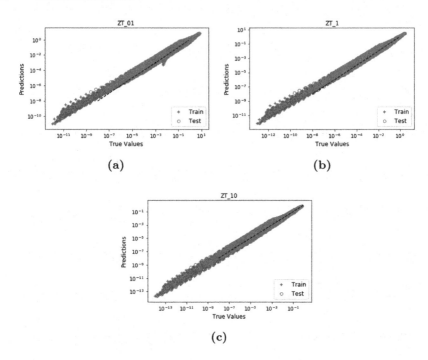

**Fig. 4. Test 2.** (a) Logarithmic plot of the predictions for $ZT_{0.1}$ on train and test set. (b) Logarithmic plot of the predictions for $ZT_1$ on train and test set. (c) Logarithmic plot of the predictions for $ZT_{10}$ on train and test set. The black dashed line is the bisector of the first quadrant.

## 4    Conclusions

We applied a very standard neural network model to the problem of predicting the thermoelectric figure of merit, the $ZT$ value, of a set of synthetic band structures corresponding to idealised unknown test materials. The dataset has been synthetically generated in order to have plenty of data, which allowed investigating the feasibility of such an approach in scenarios where large quantities of real-world data are available. The results have been very promising.

In our first test we predicted the values of $ZT$ using a completely out-of-the-box approach. While the general trend of the figure of merit was correctly identified, the quality of the predictions was somewhat coarse. This applied especially to the smaller values which, while being the least interesting quantities for the application in which this work is concerned, could still be important for other aspects.

In our second test we specialised the neural network to output only positive values. The reason behind this was the physical knowledge that the $ZT$ is a positive number. This change impacted the performance of the model very visibly, gaining accuracy in the predictions across the whole range of materials used for testing.

Our results show that a neural network approach can be a powerful tool in predicting physical properties of materials which would otherwise be very expensive to compute in classical ways, for example through a DFT approach. The application of machine learning techniques can therefore boost the research of novel energy materials by analysing large sectors of the parameters space, i.e. large quantities of chemical compounds, and providing an indication about which materials are promising candidates exhibiting high thermoelectric properties. One can then perform the expensive, but accurate, DFT laboratory tests only on those promising candidates. Machine learning approaches have therefore a very good potential to greatly increase the efficiency in the use of scientific resources. This simple but significant experiment further shows that it can be beneficial when physical prior knowledge is built-in in a machine learning model.

# References

1. United States Environmetal Protection Agency. https://www.epa.gov/chp/chp-benefits. Accessed 04 Apr 2019
2. Forman, C., Muritala, I., Pardemann, R., Meyer, B.: Estimating the global waste heat potential. Renew. Sustain. Energy Rev. **57**, 1568–1579 (2016)
3. Gayner, C., Kar, K.: Recent advances in thermoelectric materials. Prog. Mater. Sci. **83**, 330–382 (2016)
4. Løvvik, O.M., Berland, K.: Predicting the thermoelectric figure-of-merit from first principles. Mater. Today Proc. **5**, 10227–10234 (2018)
5. Parr, R.: Density functional theory of atoms and molecules. In: Horizons of Quantum Chemistry, pp. 5–15. Springer (1980). https://doi.org/10.1007/978-94-009-9027-2_2
6. Petsagkourakis, I., Tybrandt, K., Crispin, X., Ohkubo, I., Satoh, N., Mori, T.: Thermoelectric materials and applications for energy harvesting power generation. Sci. Technol. Adv. Mater. **19**(1), 836–862 (2018)
7. Schuch, N., Verstraete, F.: Computational complexity of interacting electrons and fundamental limitations of density functional theory. Nat. Phys. **5**(10), 732 (2009)
8. Shi, X., Chen, L., Uher, C.: Recent advances in high-performance bulk thermoelectric materials. Int. Mater. Rev. **61**(6), 379–415 (2016)
9. Sirusi, A., Ross, J.: Recent NMR studies of thermoelectric materials. In: Annual Reports on NMR Spectroscopy, vol. 92, pp. 137–198. Academic Press (2017)
10. Tabib, M.V., Løvvik, O.M., Johannessen, K., Rasheed, A., Sagvolden, E., Rustad, A.M.: Discovering thermoelectric materials using machine learning: insights and challenges. In: Kůrková, V., Manolopoulos, Y., Hammer, B., Iliadis, L., Maglogiannis, I. (eds.) ICANN 2018. LNCS, vol. 11139, pp. 392–401. Springer, Cham (2018). https://doi.org/10.1007/978-3-030-01418-6_39

# Data-Driven Prediction
# of Vortex-Induced Vibration Response
# of Marine Risers Subjected
# to Three-Dimensional Current

Signe Riemer-Sørensen[1]([⊠]) [iD], Jie Wu[2], Halvor Lie[2], Svein Sævik[3] [iD],
and Sang-Woo Kim[3]

[1] Department of Mathematics and Cybernetics, SINTEF Digital, Oslo, Norway
`signe.riemer-sorensen@sintef.no`
[2] Department of Energy and Transport, SINTEF Ocean, Trondheim, Norway
`{jie.wu,halvor.lie}@sintef.no`
[3] Department of Marine Technology, NTNU, Trondheim, Norway
`{svein.savik,sangwoo.kim}@ntnu.no`

**Abstract.** Slender marine structures such as deep-water marine risers are subjected to currents and will normally experience Vortex Induced Vibrations (VIV), which can cause fast accumulation of fatigue damage. The ocean current is often three-dimensional (3D), i.e., the direction and magnitude of the current vary throughout the water column.

Today, semi-empirical tools are used by the industry to predict VIV induced fatigue on risers. The load model and hydrodynamic parameters in present VIV prediction tools are developed based on two-dimensional (2D) flow conditions, as it is challenging to consider the effect of 3D flow along the risers. Accordingly, the current profiles must be purposely made 2D during the design process, which leads to significant uncertainty in the prediction results.

Further, due to the limitations in the laboratory, VIV model tests are mostly carried out under 2D flow conditions and thus little experimental data exist to document VIV response of riser subjected to varying directions of the current. However, a few experiments have been conducted with 3D current. We have used results from one of these experiments to investigate how well (1) traditional and (2) an alternative method based on a data driven prediction can describe VIV in 3D currents.

Data driven modelling is particularly suited for complicated problems with many parameters and non-linear relationships. We have applied a data clustering algorithm to the experimental 3D flow data in order to identify measurable parameters that can influence responses. The riser responses are grouped based on their statistical characteristics, which relate to the direction of the flow. Furthermore we fit a random forest regression model to the measured VIV response and compare its performance with the predictions of existing VIV prediction tools (VIVANA-FD).

© Springer Nature Switzerland AG 2019
K. Bach and M. Ruocco (Eds.): NAIS 2019, CCIS 1056, pp. 78–89, 2019.
https://doi.org/10.1007/978-3-030-35664-4_8

**Keywords:** Machine learning · Marine risers · Vortex induced vibrations

# 1 Introduction

Slender marine structures such as deep water marine risers are exposed to ocean currents causing vortices to be shed in the wake of the circular cross-section as illustrated in Fig. 1. This will cause alternating lift forces that may synchronise with the cylinder's motion such that high-frequency vibrations can occur, a phenomenon termed Vortex Induced Vibrations (VIV). The vortex shedding frequency may synchronise to a multiple set of riser eigen-frequencies. This may lead to fatigue during short exposure times even if the associated response amplitudes are small. As this limits riser lifetime, VIV are a major concern in riser design and operation.

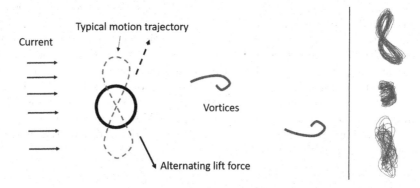

**Fig. 1.** *Left panel:* Vortex Induced Vibrations (VIV) due to vortices shed in the wake of a slender marine riser (seen from above). The VIV manifest as movements e.g. in a figure-of-eight like pattern (dashed red line). *Right panel:* Examples of riser trajectories in the x/y plane perpendicular to the length of the riser. (Color figure online)

The load model and hydrodynamic parameters in present frequency domain VIV prediction tools used by industry, i.e., VIVANA [7], Shear7 [14] and VIVA [11], are developed for the simplified 2D flow conditions. However, the speed of the current and spatial patterns in the field may vary over the water column leading to 3D flow conditions [8]. It is common practice to perform pure cross-flow VIV analysis with current profiles purposely made 2D, which is an obvious over-simplification. This is partially due to the lack of a reliable model in present VIV prediction algorithms of combined in-line and cross-flow responses. In addition, the hydrodynamic load in the frequency domain prediction tools is assumed to be harmonic, which is a simplification of the true load process (non-harmonic). A new time domain prediction tool has been developed [9,10], but systematic validation of the tool subjected to 3D flow condition is needed.

Experimental VIV model tests subjected to 2D flow have been carried out in recent years [4,12,15, e.g.]. Limited test data can be found for VIV in 3D flow conditions. The common challenge of these data is that VIV response becomes increasingly complex with many parameters that interplay and influence the physical process. Consequently, it is also difficult to model the process in a simplified mathematical model.

Data driven modelling and machine learning algorithms are powerful and highly flexible model-free methods for inferring relationships in data [3]. They are constructed to handle highly complex problems with many parameters and non-linear relationships. However, to take full advantage of the methods, high-quality data with many samples are required.

VIV response modelling is complex and model tests provide experimental data for testing the suitability of a machine learning approach (Sect. 2). First we applied unsupervised learning (clustering) to explore and identify relationships in the data in order to select the most relevant parameters from the high-dimensional data set (Sect. 3). Secondly, we used supervised learning to build a regression model that can predict the statistical properties of the VIV response based on the flow properties (Sect. 4.2).

The overall objective of the research is to obtain more accurate estimation of riser VIV fatigue damage by combining traditional prediction methods with machine learning to be integrated in future on-site riser monitoring systems. This paper presents a first attempt on the possible improvements by including the effect of 3D current in the otherwise 2D traditional VIV prediction tools. VIV response prediction is carried out with existing VIV prediction tools and compared with similar predictions from a data driven model in order to investigate the limitations and potentials of both methods.

## 2   VIV Model Test with 3D Flow

We use data from an experiment carried out in 1996 and 1997 at the MARINTEK (now part of SINTEF Ocean) towing tank using a rotating rig.

**Experimental Setup and Riser Model:** In the laboratory, 3D flow conditions were mimicked using a rotation rig as shown in Fig. 2. The rig was mounted in the deepest part of a towing tank having a length, width, and depth of 80 m, 10.5 m and 10 m, respectively. The test rig consisted of a 13 m long vertical cylinder with a diameter of about 0.5 m. Bearings in both ends of the cylinder made it possible to rotate the rig around its vertical axis by use of an electrical actuator. The rotating cylinder was mounted with horizontal arms at the top and bottom. The riser model was suspended between these arms in a pretension arrangement. At the lower connection point it had a constant arm length of 4.6 m. The upper connection arm length could be varied from 0.4 m to 4.6 m.

During the test, the rig was rotated around the vertical cylinder at constant rotational velocity. Thus, the riser experienced a water flow given by the rotational speed and distance to the rotational axis. For equal arm lengths, the flow

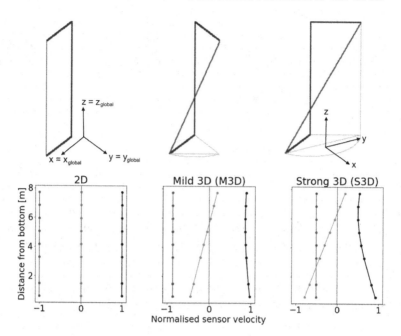

**Fig. 2.** *Upper panel:* The geometrical configuration of the arms (blue) and the riser (red). In the 2D configuration (left), the angle between the horizontal arms was 0° leading to a 2D flow. In the mild 3D configuration (middle) the angle between the arms was 60° and in the strong 3D configuration (left) the angle was 120°, both leading to a 3D sheared flow. *Lower panel:* Normalised velocities along the riser in the x-direction ($u_x/U$, blue), y-direction ($u_y/U$, orange), and magnitude of total velocity ($u_{tot}/U$, black thick line), where $U$ refers to the velocity of the tip of the lower arm. (Color figure online)

speed was uniform in magnitude and direction along the riser model. Decreasing the upper arm length, led to a variation in the flow along the riser model, resulting in a sheared, but still 2D, flow. More detailed description of the test set-up can be found in [5].

In order to accommodate 3D flow conditions, the planar angle between the upper and lower arms could be adjusted. When the two arms were offset, the current flow varied in direction along the riser model. Hence, it was possible to test a riser model subjected to a well-defined 3D current profile. Seven different setup set-up configurations were performed, where the length of the upper arm varied between 2.7 m to 4.6 m, and the angle between the horizontal arms varied between 0° and 165°. In the present study only the three configurations with constant upper arm length of 4.6 m were included. The angle between the arms were 0°, 60° and 120°, resulting in a uniform 2D current profile, a mild 3D current profile and a strong 3D current profile.

The outer diameter of the test model riser was 23 mm with a weight in water of $1.433\,\mathrm{Nm^{-1}}$. The riser had been modified to house accelerometers, and stiffened

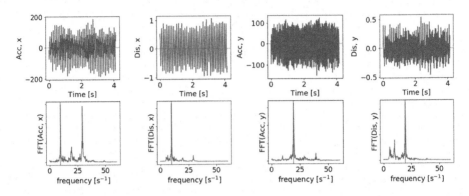

**Fig. 3.** An example of a time series interval for sensor 5 in the 2D geometry with rotational velocity of $1.629\,\mathrm{ms}^{-1}$ in the sample interval 5000 to 5500. The upper panels show the time series and the lower panels the real part of the fast Fourier transform.

with a 4 mm steel wire to obtain a high axial elastic stiffness and strength. It was filled with gelatin to avoid vibrations of the cabling inside.

**Time Series:** The response of the riser was measured with 10 pairs of bi-axial accelerometers mounted along the length of the riser. The accelerations were measured along and perpendicular to the length of the riser with a sampling frequency of 120 Hz. During the tests two of the accelerometers (number 3 and 10 from the bottom) failed and were rejected from further analysis.

The measured accelerations were Fourier transformed and low-pass filtered at 30 Hz to remove high frequency noise, before being doubly integrated in the frequency domain to obtain displacement time series. The transient phase in the measured signals at the beginning and the end of each test case were discarded so the total signal consisted of time steps from 2500 to 8000 (21.8–66.7 s). We split the time series in intervals of 500 samples corresponding to 4.2 s an example of which is given in Fig. 3. We used a fast Fourier transform of the time intervals to get the dominating oscillation frequencies (lower panels of Fig. 3).

We only considered local current and treated each sensor and each time interval as independent measurements. This is a strong simplification since it is known that VIV responses will be correlated over the length of the riser model.

The inaccuracy of the accelerometers and other sensors was a few percent of the true values. In addition, it is observed that VIV response is not completely stationary. Therefore, the standard deviation of the measured response can vary depending on the time slot. For the total displacement, the deviation between the time slots can be up to 15%.

**Features:** In total we considered the features listed in Table 1. They are not independent and at different stages in the analysis different subsets were selected as specified.

**Table 1.** The full set of considered features. The x- and y-directions refer to the plane perpendicular to the length of the riser (see Fig. 2)

| Feature | Explanation |
|---|---|
| $\sigma_{Acc,x}$, $\sigma_{Acc,y}$ | Standard deviation of acceleration in the x, y directions in $ms^{-2}$ |
| $\gamma_{Acc,x}$, $\gamma_{Acc,y}$ | Skewness of acceleration in the x, y direction, no units |
| $\kappa_{Acc,x}$, $\kappa_{Acc,y}$ | Kurtosis of acceleration in the x, y direction, no units |
| $\sigma_{Dis,x}$, $\sigma_{Dis,y}$ | Standard deviation of displacement divided by riser diameter |
| $\sigma_{tot}$ | Standard deviation of total displacement divided by riser diameter |
| $\gamma_{Dis,x}$, $\gamma_{Dis,y}$ | Skewness of displacement in the x, y direction, no units |
| $\kappa_{Dis,x}$, $\kappa_{Dis,y}$ | Kurtosis of displacement in the x, y direction, no units |
| $f_{Dis,x}$, $f_{Dis,y}$ | Frequency of oscillations in x, y direction in units of $s^{-1}$ |
| $u_{tot}$ | Total sensor velocity (equal to current) in $ms^{-1}$ |
| $u_x$, $u_y$ | Magnitude of sensor velocity in the x, y direction in $ms^{-1}$ |
| $U$ | Velocity of lower arm in $ms^{-1}$ |
| $d$ | Sensor distance from bottom in m |

In addition to the variance (standard deviation) of the distributions, we also regarded skewness and kurtosis. Skewness is the third standardised central moment for the probability distribution. It describes the symmetry of the distribution. Kurtosis is the fourth standardised central moment of the probability distribution. It is a measure of the combined weights of the tails relative to the rest of the distribution [16]. Vandiver [13] used kurtosis to characterise the VIV responses. It assumes a value of 1.5 for a sinusoidal process as typical for a single mode lock-in response, and a value of 3.0 for a Gaussian process typical for multi-frequency random vibration.

## 3   Clustering

We used unsupervised learning to investigate the relations between the dimensionality of the current and the statistical properties of the oscillations. In order to focus on the flow dimensionality, we only considered measurements where the total sensor velocity fell within a narrow range, $u_{tot} = 1.1-1.2\,ms^{-1}$.

**Hierarchical Density Based Clustering:** Clustering basically means sorting the data points according to similarities in the full parameter space. For a few features this can easily be visualised, but for many features visualisation is challenging.

Hierarchical density based clustering uses the density of the points in feature space to build cluster trees hierarchically. The tree is then condensed based on a minimum cluster size [2,6]. Contrary to other clustering methods, the user does not specify a number of clusters, but instead specifies the minimal cluster size.

The points that do not fulfil the criteria for becoming a cluster are assigned to a noise/outlier category. The user can control the conservatism of the clustering i.e. how strict the algorithm should be when assigning points to clusters or noise. Density based scanning is particularly good at handing elongated and overlapping clusters, and due to the noise option it is suitable for exploratory data analysis.

**Method and Results of Clustering:** We applied hierarchical density based clustering to the full set of features in Table 1 with Euclidian distance as similarity matrix, minimum cluster size of 18 members, and minimum number of samples (the conservatism) of 1. Since the data were equally distributed among the three scenarios with different governing physics, we expected the clusters to be small and homogeneous, and consequently we used the leaf method for cluster selection (rather than the default mass excess method which has a tendency to produce large clusters).

The importance of individual features in the clustering combined with physical reasoning and correlations between the features were used to select a subset of relevant features consisting of: $\sigma_{Acc,x}$, $\sigma_{Acc,y}$, $\kappa_{Acc,x}$, $\kappa_{Acc,y}$, $f_{Dis,x}$, $f_{Dis,y}$, $u_x$, $u_y$.

The upper panel of Fig. 4 shows the parameter distributions for each of the clusters. The randomly selected cluster members shown in the lower panels have visually similar trajectories. Consequently, the statistical information is descriptive of the physical scenario, and can be used by the clustering algorithm do distinguish between the scenarios.

**Other Clustering Methods:** In addition to the density based clustering, we tested other methods such as Gaussian Mixture and Agglomerative clustering. Gaussian mixture clustering is a generalisation of k-means clustering where it is assumed that all data points are generated from a mixture of a finite number of overlapping Gaussian probability distributions. Agglomerative clustering is a bottom-up hierarchical clustering approach, where each data point starts as its own cluster, and the clusters are subsequently merged. When using only the parameters that have a high significance in the density based clustering, the results of the three methods are very similar.

## 4   Response Prediction

Given the clear correlation between oscillation pattern, configuration and statistical parameters, it should be possible to use supervised learning to predict the statistical properties of the response from a simple input.

The end goal is to predict the long term fatigue for realistic current profiles. Since the fatigue is strongly dependent on the response, we simplify the problem and here we compare the response prediction from traditional methods, such as VIVANA-FD, with a data driven random forest learning approach. We randomly

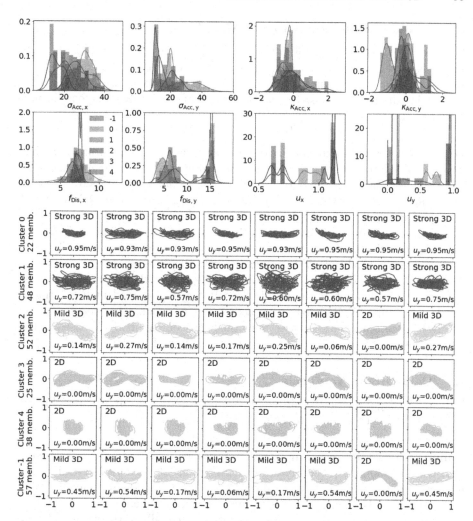

**Fig. 4.** *Upper panel:* Distributions of the statistical parameters of the clusters. The bars show the normalised histograms while the thin lines are the kernel density estimates. The cluster numbers correspond to the cluster members shown below. *Lower panel:* Examples of trajectories of cluster members. The colours and labels indicate the configuration. The last row shows examples of data points that are assigned to the noise category. The clusters are derived based on statistical properties of the accelerations and displacements, and not the trajectories shown here. The fact that the cluster members have visually similar trajectories indicate that the statistical parameters are descriptive of the physical scenarios. (Color figure online)

selected a test case in the strong 3D configuration with bottom flow speed of $U_{\text{tot}} = 1.105\,\text{ms}^{-1}$ and sampling interval 2500–3000 for comparison.

## 4.1   Traditional Method with VIVANA-FD

The flow speed varies in magnitude and direction along the length of the riser model as shown in Fig. 2 (normalised by total flow speed). The empirical frequency domain VIV prediction program VIVANA-FD was used for the case study using discrete response frequencies. The equation of dynamic equilibrium is defined as

$$M\ddot{r} + C\dot{r} + Kr = R, \tag{1}$$

where $R$ represents the external forces, $M$ incorporates the structural and hydrodynamic added mass, $C$ describes structural and hydrodynamic damping, and $K$ is the stiffness matrix. $M$, $C$ and $R$ are functions of the response vector $r$, which necessitates an iterative solution scheme. It is assumed that the excitation and response are harmonic at identical frequencies. This type of stationary response is assumed by most of the empirical VIV softwares [7,11,14]. The main hydrodynamic coefficients are the added mass, excitation and damping coefficients, which are generalised from VIV model test with 2D flows.

The 3D flow is normally converted to 2D by using the total velocity. The displacement prediction with the 2D flow profile is presented in Fig. 5 (lower panel, green line). VIVANA-FD predicts a single response frequency ($f_{osc} = 6.87\,\text{Hz}$) to dominate the responses along the length of riser model. Consequently, the response will be harmonic due to the assumption of the load model.

## 4.2   Data Driven Approach

Instead of using a physics-based model, the purpose of data driven modelling is to fit the data with a highly flexible model.

**Random Forest Regression:** Random forest regression is based on decision trees with a technique called bootstrap aggregation (also known as bagging) [1]. Rather than using individual decision trees, the data is randomly sampled (with replacement) and a decision tree is trained for each sample.

In order for each feature/variable to contribute equally to the fitting process, the input and output features must be scaled individually to the same range. We performed a min-max scaling to the range [0, 1], before randomly splitting the data into a training sample (80%) and a test sample (20%). The input parameters were $d$, $u_{tot}$, $u_x$, $u_y$, and the output parameters were the remaining parameters in Table 1. However, there was a clear connection between the parameters with an important role in the clustering, and the parameters that could be well determined with the random forest model, so we restricted the output to $\sigma_{Dis,x}$, $\sigma_{Dis,y}$, $f_{Dis,x}$, $f_{Dis,y}$, $\sigma_{tot}$.

We used a grid search to optimise the hyper-parameters to a depth of 10 layers in the decision trees and 400 estimators. For a 5-fold cross validation, the best mean squared error on the normalised training data was 0.0062 and 0.0060 on the normalised test data. That the model performed better on the test data than the training data is a good sign that it was not over-fitting. For the individual parameters the mean square error was varying from 0.002 to 0.009.

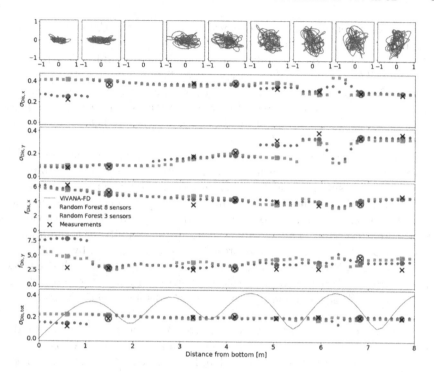

**Fig. 5.** *Top panel:* Trajectories of the case study; the strong 3D configuration with a bottom flow speed of $1.105\,\text{ms}^{-1}$ for sample range 2500–3000. *Subsequent panels:* The measurements (black crosses) and model predictions for the case study. The blue circles show the random forest prediction from fitting to data from all sensors with the sensor positions highlighted as larger circles. The orange squares show the predictions from fitting only three sensors (highlighted as red circles), but predicting for all sensors. The *lowest panel* shows the standard deviation of the displacement (in units of riser diameter). The green line is the prediction from VIVANA-FD assuming 2D flow. (Color figure online)

## 4.3  Results and Comparison

Figure 5 shows the results of both predictive approaches compared to the measurements of the strong 3D configuration with bottom flow speed of $U_{\text{tot}} = 1.105\,\text{ms}^{-1}$ (excluded from training and test samples). As discussed in Sect. 2, the measured variation of displacement may vary up to 15% between the time intervals, and hence it is a reasonable estimate of the uncertainty on the measured displacement amplitudes plotted in the lowest panel of Fig. 5.

Visually, the random forest model (blue) provide good predictions at the sensor locations. The sensor closest to the bottom is also closest to the pinned end. Consequently, it will have smaller displacements and the measurements are more prone to noise. Further analysis is required to identify the origin of the discrepancy and possible improvements of the model at this location. Around 6–7 m from the bottom there is an "oscillation" in the model, mostly pronounced for $\sigma_{\text{Dis,y}}$. Since there are no measurements between the accelerometers, it is uncertain whether this is an artefact of the model but the feature remains when fitting the model to fewer sensors.

Deep-water risers will normally have a limited number of sensors. Hence we tested the ability of the model to interpolate by fitting only to data from a sub-sample of the sensors (orange in Fig. 5) but predicting the response at all sensor locations. The three-sensor fit leads to larger deviations than fitting all sensors, but still with decent performance, in particular for the predictions of the total displacement (lowest panel in Fig. 5).

The lowest panel in Fig. 5 shows the variation of the total displacement. The VIVANA-FD prediction (green line) over-predicts the displacement amplitude relative to the measurements along the entire riser leading to a root mean squared error of 4.8 relative to the measurements at the sensor locations. In addition, the predicted response is harmonic compared to the almost flat behaviour of the measured responses. The explanation lies in the simplifying assumptions of VIVANA-FD. Firstly, the predicted responses are dominated by a single frequency leading to harmonic oscillations. This is contrary to the multi-frequency responses observed in the measurements (shown in Fig. 3). Secondly, the 2D assumption clearly leads to over-prediction of the displacement amplitude.

The random fores prediction is closer to the data both when fitted to all data (root mean squared error of 0.02 relative to sensor measurements) and to a reduced set of sensors. In the present case study, the VIVANA-FD model is significantly less accurate than the random forest model. This not surprising as it has been derived for a simplified scenario with 2D current but is compared to a 3D current scenario. However, the data driven method requires realistic training data, and without further information about the system, it cannot easily be transferred to e.g. a different type of riser. The ideal solution will be to combine the methods into a hybrid solution in order to obtain high precision and transferability.

## 5   Summary and Conclusion

Using density based clustering we found a clear relation between dimensionality of the current and the observed pattern of riser movement and consequently fatigue. The response pattern can be identified from the statistical properties of the movement alone. We fitted a random forest model for the statistical parameters based on the local current conditions and position on the riser. The random forest model provide a more precise prediction of the displacement amplitude ($\sigma_{tot}$) than the traditional approach using VIVANA-FD. However, as it is completely data driven, it does not provide any insights on the physics behind the riser response, and in order to translate the random forest model between different riser types and scale it to operational risers, additional training data is required spanning all relevant scenarios. The natural way forward is to combine the physics based modelling with the data driven approach in a hybrid solution.

**Acknowledgements.** The authors would like to thank Anne Marthine Rustad for discussions and suggestions. This study was sponsored by Equinor, BP, Kongsberg Maritime, Trelleborg Offshore, Aker Solutions and Subsea7.

# References

1. Breiman, L.: Random forests. Mach. Learn. **45**(1), 5–32 (2001). https://doi.org/10.1023/A:1010933404324
2. Campello, R.J.G.B., Moulavi, D., Sander, J.: Density-based clustering based on hierarchical density estimates. In: Pei, J., Tseng, V.S., Cao, L., Motoda, H., Xu, G. (eds.) PAKDD 2013. LNCS (LNAI), vol. 7819, pp. 160–172. Springer, Heidelberg (2013). https://doi.org/10.1007/978-3-642-37456-2_14
3. Hastie, T., Tibshirani, R., Friedman, J.H.: The Elements of Statistical Learning: Data Mining, Inference, and Prediction. Springer Series in Statistics, 2nd edn. Springer, New York (2009). https://doi.org/10.1007/978-0-387-84858-7. http://www.worldcat.org/oclc/300478243
4. Lie, H., Braaten, H., Jhingran, V., Sequeiros, O.E., Vandiver, K.: Comprehensive riser VIV model tests in uniform and sheared flow. In: 31st International Conference on Ocean, Offshore and Arctic Engineering, ASME 2012, vol. 5 (2012). https://doi.org/10.1115/OMAE2012-84055
5. Lie, H., Mo, K., Vandiver, J.: VIV model test of a bare- and a staggered buoyancy riser in a rotating rig. In: Offshore Technology Conference, OTC-8700-MS, Houston, Texas (1998). https://doi.org/10.4043/8700-MS
6. McInnes, L., Healy, J., Astels, S.: HDBSCAN: hierarchical density based clustering. J. Open Source Softw. **2**(11) (2017). https://doi.org/10.21105/joss.00205
7. Passano, E., Larsen, C., Lie, H., Wu, J.: VIVANA - Theory Manual Version 4.4 (2014)
8. Srivilairit, T., Manuel, L.: Vortex-induced vibration and coincident current velocity profiles for a deepwater drilling riser. J. Offshore Mech. Arct. Eng. **131**, 021101 (2009). https://doi.org/10.1115/1.3058684
9. Thorsen, M., Sævik, S., Larsen, C.: A simplified method for time domain simulation of cross-flow vortex-induced vibrations. J. Fluids Struct. **49**, 135–148 (2014). https://doi.org/10.1016/j.jfluidstructs.2014.04.006
10. Thorsen, M., Sævik, S., Larsen, C.: Non-linear time domain analysis of cross-flow vortex-induced vibrations. Mar. Struct. **51**, 134–151 (2017). https://doi.org/10.1016/j.marstruc.2016.10.007
11. Triantafyllou, M., Triantafyllou, G., Tein, Y.D., Ambrose, B.D.: Pragmatic riser VIV analysis. In: Offshore Technology Conference, OTC-10931-MS, Houston, Texas (1999). https://doi.org/10.4043/10931-MS
12. Trim, A., Braaten, H., Lie, H., Tognarelli, M.: Experimental investigation of vortex-induced vibration of long marine risers. J. Fluids Struct. **21**(3), 335–361 (2005). https://doi.org/10.1016/j.jfluidstructs.2005.07.014. Marine and Aeronautical Fluid-Structure Interactions
13. Vandiver, J.: Predicting lock-in on drilling risers in sheared flows. In: Flow-Induced Vibration Conference, Lucerne, Switzerland (2000)
14. Vandiver, J., Li, L.: Shear7 v4.5 Program Theoretical Manual (2007)
15. Vandiver, J.K., Swithenbank, S.B., Jaiswal, V., Jhingran, V.: Fatigue damage from high mode number vortex-induced vibration. In: 25th International Conference on Ocean, Offshore and Arctic Engineering, ASME 2006, vol. 4 (2006). https://doi.org/10.1115/OMAE2006-92409
16. Westfall, P.H.: Kurtosis as peakedness, 1905–2014. R.I.P. Am. Stat. **68**(3), 191–195 (2014). https://doi.org/10.1080/00031305.2014.917055

# Energy Industry Perspective on the Definition of Autonomy for Mobile Robots

Francesco Scibilia[1]([⊠]), Knut Sebastian Tungland[2], Anders Røyrøy[3], and Marianne Bryhni Asla[4]

[1] Equinor AS, Trondheim, Norway
fsci@equinor.com
[2] Equinor AS, Stavanger, Norway
ktun@equinor.com
[3] Equinor AS, Bergen, Norway
aroy@equinor.com
[4] Equinor AS, Kårstø, Tysværvåg, Norway
mba@equinor.com

**Abstract.** Autonomy refers to a system that decides and performs actions motivated by some intended objectives, and those actions are justifiable by sound reasoning with respect to these objectives. Artificial intelligence (AI) is here intended as the technology that enables autonomy. Artificially intelligent autonomous robots are predicted to play an increasingly important role in the energy industry capability to address the society demand for energy. The development of such advanced systems needs to start with defining AI and autonomy for asset owners in the energy industry. In general, different applications will require different engineering definitions of AI and different levels of autonomy.

**Keywords:** Autonomy · Artificial intelligence · Mobile robots · Energy industry

## 1 Introduction

The energy industry is sustained by support functions as monitoring, inspection and maintenance of capital intensive and long service life assets. These support functions ensure safe and optimal operations of complex installations and highly engineered assets, and imply often works at heights, underwater, under chemical exposure, in restrained spaces, or in explosive environments. Performing such functions in remote locations as offshore and/or on a 24/7 response capability, makes it for an even more resource intensive activity.

The value potential of autonomous robots in the energy industry is enormous [1, 2].

## 2 Artificially Intelligent Autonomous Robots

In general, autonomy needs to be differentiated from automation. Automation refers to a system that does exactly what it is programmed to do, without choice or possibility to

© Springer Nature Switzerland AG 2019
K. Bach and M. Ruocco (Eds.): NAIS 2019, CCIS 1056, pp. 90–101, 2019.
https://doi.org/10.1007/978-3-030-35664-4_9

act in any different way. Instead, autonomy refers to a system that decides and performs actions motivated by some intended objectives, and those actions are justifiable by sound reasoning with respect to these objectives. Artificial intelligence (AI) is here intended as the technology that enables autonomy.

Many definitions of AI have been proposed in the literature [3] reflecting different aspects and perspectives. However, most often the given definition remains at a rather academic and general level to be used directly for an engineering design process. An interesting definition is "AI is the attempt to get the machine to do things that, for the moment, people are better at" [4]. This definition implies that once a task is performed successfully by a machine, then that technology becomes no longer AI. Another interesting definition is "AI is creating machines that perform functions that require intelligence when performed by people" [5]. This definition implies that only tasks that requires human intelligence in order to be solved are defining AI. Combining these two definitions one could define autonomy for robots as "Autonomy is creating a robot to perform non-trivial functions that, for the moment, people are better at." This definition highlights an important aspect for the industry. Autonomy is not an ultimate technology state to aim for, it is rather a continuous improvement process that empowers the company human resources to tackle complex challenges more efficiently. This continuous improvement process is formed by a sequence of stepping stones that brings incremental value to the business.

However, this definition is still not suited for a direct engineering design process. In fact, an engineering definition of autonomy cannot be given without considering a specific task and application domain, and it will in general differ from task to task, domain to domain. For example, the automotive industry defines autonomy as "an autonomous car is a vehicle that can travel between destinations without a human operator". However, it easy to see that transferring this definition to equipment inspection applications, for example, will not be sufficient: a robot able to move from A to B without a human operator will certainly be a valuable and advanced solution, but it cannot be said to be an autonomous inspection solution since the inspection goal is not achieved by simply having the robot at a certain position. This is obvious if one considers autonomy of complex assets in the energy industry as offshore production platforms. Full autonomous production in this case entails autonomy of many interconnected functions and systems (Fig. 1). In general, here the way to full autonomy starts from the functions at the base of the hierarchy, climbing to higher functions as autonomy is achieved; as functions higher in the pyramid are considered, implementing full autonomy becomes more involved and challenging.

This aspect is also relevant if one considers simpler systems as an unmanned ground vehicle or an unmanned aerial vehicle. In fact, these robots may be performing their tasks on an offshore production platform and will have to integrate to existing systems, procedures, processes and operate among and together human operators.

The requirement of autonomous robot to work with human operators highlights another relevant aspect. Full autonomy in the automotive domain implies removing the human completely from the loop. Instead, for applications in the energy industry

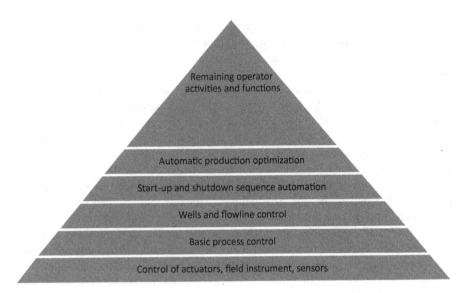

**Fig. 1.** Hierarchy view of main functions in production platforms

autonomous robots are most often part of a process at the top of which there is a responsible human operator. Autonomous robots are intended as empowering the skilled human workforce. Therefore, it is more appropriate to follow a human-robot interaction (HRI) [6] approach in the definition of autonomy. Implications of an HRI approach are that the autonomous robot design should ensure that the human operator is never removed from the overall command role. The decisions and actions taken by the autonomous robot should be comprehensible to the operator, and the robot system should support situation awareness. The autonomous system should be designed taking into due consideration that the operator will become reliant on the system correct functioning.

## 3   Levels of Autonomy

One of the most important aspects to consider is that autonomy is in general not a binary property, a robot is not either autonomous or not. Instead, it is more appropriate to talk about Levels of Autonomy (LoA). As an engineering definition of autonomy depends on the specific application, so does the engineering definition of levels of autonomy.

In general, the levels of autonomy describe to what degree a robot is capable to act on its own accord. Different definitions of LoA have been proposed in the literature, a comprehensive review can be found in [7]. In the following we consider only a selection of LoA definitions to highlight key aspects.

A popular example today of LoA is the one given by the Society of Automotive Engineers (SAE) for the automotive industry [8] (Fig. 2):

| SAE level | Name | Narrative Definition | Execution of Steering and Acceleration/ Deceleration | Monitoring of Driving Environment | Fallback Performance of Dynamic Driving Task | System Capability (Driving Modes) |
|---|---|---|---|---|---|---|
| *Human driver* monitors the driving environment | | | | | | |
| 0 | No Automation | the full-time performance by the *human driver* of all aspects of the *dynamic driving task*, even when enhanced by warning or intervention systems | Human driver | Human driver | Human driver | n/a |
| 1 | Driver Assistance | the *driving mode*-specific execution by a driver assistance system of either steering or acceleration/deceleration using information about the driving environment and with the expectation that the *human driver* perform all remaining aspects of the *dynamic driving task* | Human driver and system | Human driver | Human driver | Some driving modes |
| 2 | Partial Automation | the *driving mode*-specific execution by one or more driver assistance systems of both steering and acceleration/deceleration using information about the driving environment and with the expectation that the *human driver* perform all remaining aspects of the dynamic driving task | System | Human driver | Human driver | Some driving modes |
| *Automated driving system* ("*system*") monitors the driving environment | | | | | | |
| 3 | Conditional Automation | the *driving mode*-specific performance by an *automated driving system* of all aspects of the dynamic driving task with the expectation that the *human driver* will respond appropriately to a *request to intervene* | System | System | Human driver | Some driving modes |
| 4 | High Automation | the *driving mode*-specific performance by an automated driving system of all aspects of the *dynamic driving task* even if a human driver does not respond appropriately to a *request to intervene* | System | System | System | Some driving modes |
| 5 | Full Automation | the full-time performance by an *automated driving system* of all aspects of the *dynamic driving task* under all roadway and environmental conditions that can be managed by a human driver | System | System | System | All driving modes |

**Fig. 2.** SAE levels of autonomy in the automotive industry

The 6 levels span from no automation to full automation of the so-called dynamic driving task, which includes operational (as steering, acceleration) and tactical (as determining when to turn, change lines) features of driving. Note how the car system takes increasingly more responsibility over the driver as the LoA increases, with key point between level 2 and 3 where the system takes over the responsibility to monitor the driving environment. At level 4 the system is responsible to perform fallback manoeuvres to counteract unexpected events or failures.

Another relevant definition of autonomy with high focus on safe operations is the one related to autonomous ships [9]. Ship autonomy types (Fig. 3) are defined as function of autonomy levels and bridge manning level. Moreover, the definition of autonomy for ships needs to consider all the support systems to navigation and the general operational context. It is important to note here that full autonomy does not mean complete independence from human operator, in fact in almost all cases the ship is expected to be remotely supervised from a remote control centre.

One of the most well-known definition to measure the autonomy of a system is the Sheridan's scale of levels of autonomy [10].

The 10 levels of autonomy given by Sheridan (Table 1) are focused on machine decision-making and execution, moving from level 1 where the human has full responsibility, to levels 2–4 concerned with who takes the decision, then levels 5–9 dealing

| | Manned bridge | Unmanned bridge - crew on board | Unmanned bridge - no crew on board |
|---|---|---|---|
| Decision support | Direct control No autonomy | Remote control | Remote control |
| Automatic | Automatic bridge | Automatic ship | Automatic ship |
| Constrained autonomous | - | Constrained autonomous | Constrained autonomous |
| Fully autonomous | - | - | Fully autonomous |

**Fig. 3.** Ship autonomy types (from [9])

with mode of execution, and to level 10 where the system is completely independent from the human (it does not even inform the human).

**Table 1.** Sheridan's levels of autonomy

| (1) | The computer offers no assistance, human must do it all |
|---|---|
| (2) | The computer offers a complete set of action alternatives, and |
| (3) | Narrows the selection down to a few, or |
| (4) | Suggests one, and |
| (5) | Executes that suggestion if the human approves, or |
| (6) | Allows the human a restricted time to veto before automatic execution, or |
| (7) | Executes automatically, then necessarily informs the human, or |
| (8) | Informs him after execution only if he asks, or |
| (9) | Informs him after execution if it, the computer, decides to |
| (10) | The computer decides everything and acts autonomously, ignoring the human |

Another notable definition based on system capability to perform functions is based on the Boyd's OODA (Observe, Orient, Decide, and Act) loop, which is a description of the human process of decision-making [11]. This approach has been used in the space industry to define the levels of autonomy required for a mission, and then to design the system according to those requirements. The use of the Boyd's system has the advantage to include feedback and implicit control concepts into the definition. Eight levels of autonomy are defined, each level describing the requirement within function types: the Observe function referring to gathering, monitoring and filtering data; the Orient function referring to deriving a list of options through analysis, trend predictions, interpretations and integrations; the Decide function referring to decision-making based on ranking of available options; and the Act function referring to execution and authority to act on the chosen options.

Another well-known definition more focused on unmanned mobile robots is the Autonomy Levels for Unmanned Systems (ALFUS) framework [12]. The ALFUS framework (Fig. 4) is the result of a collaboration of military and civilian practitioners, and defines autonomy based on the system capability to integrate sensing, perceive, analyse, communicate, plan, make decisions, and execute such to achieve its goal.

**Fig. 4.** ALFUS framework, contextual autonomous capability model

It is important to note that the ALFUS framework measures autonomy along 3 dimensions: mission complexity, environment complexity, and required human independence.

A similar multi-dimensional approach to define levels of autonomy is given by [13], where the autonomy capability of a robot is represented as an automation state in a two dimensional matrix: the row of this matrix representing the level of autonomy; the column representing the level of intelligence. In this approach, the level of autonomy indicates how much authority the robot has in taking actions, while the level of intelligence describes to which sophistication the robot is able to process information.

The importance of the HRI aspect for the definition of autonomy has been already mentioned in Sect. 2. Designing systems with increasing levels of autonomy needs to consider elements as nature of information exchange between human and robots, structure of the task and the team, adaptation, learning and training of people (and robot). Levels of autonomy with a focus on HRI consider teleoperation as the lowest level, increasing then to mediated teleoperation, supervisory control, collaborative control and then peer-to-peer collaboration as the highest level [6]. It is important to consider that higher levels of autonomy involve typically larger amounts of data and information produced and managed. This requires more sophisticated human-robot interfaces and system integration such to address issues as risk of excessive cognitive load on the operator and requirements of appropriate cognitive skills on the system for effective operator-robot interaction.

## 4 Energy Industry Asset Owner Perspective

As described in [7], many different approaches and definitions of levels of autonomy have been proposed in the literature. The authors in [7] also propose a table where all the different LOA definitions considered are compared (Fig. 5).

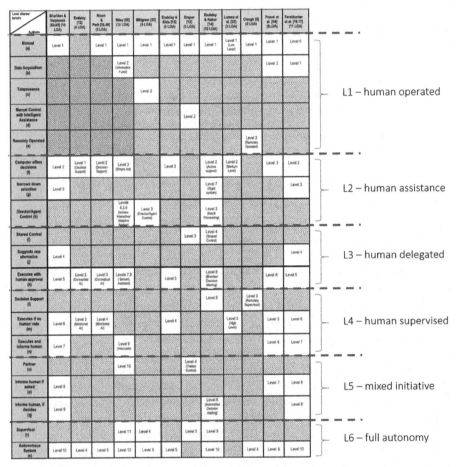

**Fig. 5.** Comparison LoA table from [7], with clustering in 6 main levels of autonomy

From the comparison in Fig. 5 it is possible to note that all the given characteristics that define autonomy levels can be clustered around six main levels (Table 2):

**Table 2.** Six levels of autonomy and corresponding HRI level.

| LoA | Name | HRI level | Description |
|---|---|---|---|
| 1 | The robot is **human operated** | Teleoperation | Full manual control, the robot visualizes information to support |
| 2 | The robot is **human assistance** | Mediated teleoperation | Manual control with robot assistance, the robot visualizes processed information to support decisions |
| 3 | The robot is **human delegated** | Supervisory control (function level) | Basic form of supervisory control, the operator activates functions that are executed by the robot. The robot process information and provides list of options |
| 4 | The robot is **human supervised** | Supervisory control (task level) | The operator is in the loop, but the robot executes the task. The robot provides necessary information for performance assessment, and option to veto |
| 5 | The robot and the human share **mixed-initiative** | Collaborative control | The operator does not need to be in the loop all the time. The robot executes the task and informs only if requested to |
| 6 | The robot has **full autonomy** | Peer-to-peer collaboration | The operator does not need to be in the loop. The robot executes the task |

The LoA description in Table 2 considers a single robot. However, higher levels of autonomy enable for multi-robot system applications, where a possibly heterogeneous collection of autonomous mobile robots works together to achieve common goals. Significant benefits and advantages are expected from multi-robot systems as: increased overall system robustness and reliability, increased capabilities, increased reactivity and speed.

To clarify the terminology used in this paper, a function is a process that changes the state of the robot and its environment, which includes sensing and data gathering. Functions can be combined to form a more complex function. A task refers to the execution of a potentially complex function characterized by a start and an end. Task performance can be typically measured at the end of execution. A mission refers to the operation assigned to a team of which the robot is part of and can be composed by different tasks. To exemplify, a team can be composed by the asset operator, the robot pilot and the robot; or by the asset operator and the autonomous robot.

To consider autonomy and the levels of autonomy from an energy industry asset owner perspective, one must have clear the role of the asset owner in the autonomous robotics market and what are the asset owner priorities.

Being the core business the production and sale of energy, the asset owner has clearly the end-user role in the robotics market. From an asset owner point of view, the main drivers for the use of robots and autonomous systems can be categorized under three main areas: Safety and security; Effectiveness and efficiency; Data value management. These priorities interplay among each other to define each level of autonomy. Moreover, the levels of autonomy are influenced by the needs for increasing system integrability and for adaptability. However, while the end-user role of the asset owner in the robotics market is easy to see, it should be also considered that asset owner aim to ensure its priorities can position the asset owner to play other important roles in the robotics market, for example as system integrator and/or operation control responsible.

Another aspect to highlight is that a fully autonomous robot designed to perform a single task in a fixed, well-modelled environment will be different than a fully autonomous robot designed to perform different tasks in a diversity of environments, with a range of interactions. The latter autonomous robot needs in fact deliberation capabilities [14], which means the robot ability to reason, justify and perform actions with respect to some intended objectives.

Putting together all the aspects considered so far, from an energy industry asset owner perspective it is more appropriate to look at the levels of autonomy as multidimensional. Here we propose the definition of autonomy to extends in at least three directions (Fig. 6).

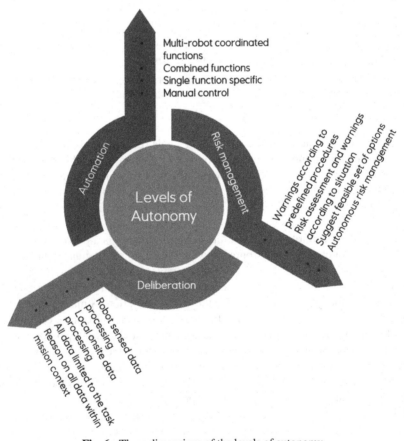

**Fig. 6.** Three dimensions of the levels of autonomy

## 4.1  Machine Operation/Automation

This dimension indicates the capability of the robot to execute functions without the need of operator intervention. Generally, a function implies a process that takes as input the robot sensing data and generates the best action according to desired references or commands. The functions are executed exactly as programmed by the programmer, the robot has no possibility to perform any differently than how designed to at the beginning. Increasing machine operation/automation capabilities can be illustrated by the following scale:

1. The robot is fully manually operated.
2. The robot can execute single specific functions.
3. The robot can combine functions to execute complex functions.
4. The robot can coordinate and collaborate with other robots/equipment to execute complex functions.

## 4.2  Risk Management

The risk management dimension indicates the capability of the robotic system to handle extreme conditions and/or system failures without operator intervention. This can be considered as making the robotic system an active and conscious risk preventive/recovery barrier. Increasing risk management capabilities can be illustrated by the following scale:

1. The robot warns the operator when approaching limits of design operating envelope.
2. The robot continuously assesses the risk and adjust warnings accordingly.
3. The robot assesses risk/events and provides list of preventive/mitigation options.
4. The robot is capable to deciding the best risk management policy.

## 4.3  Data Integration/Deliberation

Data integration/deliberation indicates the capability of the robotic system to integrate data from different sources and to deliberate with respect to intended objectives. Increasing capabilities here can be illustrated by the following scale:

1. The system analyses onboard robot sensor data and provides the operator with information relevant for the task.
2. The system analyses data from all connected devices in the same physical environment, extract relevant information, decide on adjusting desired references accordingly.
3. The system analyses distributed and historic data, makes predictions and compares with observations, decide on adjusting plans accordingly.
4. The system can reason on distributed and heterogeneous data, perform high level planning and learn from experience.

Note that here the three dimensions represent characteristics of the robot, differently than the ALFUS approach where the dimensions are defined by the environment, the mission and the required human interaction. The multidimensional approach here presented puts the definition of autonomy and LoA closer to a robot design context. We also do not exclude that there may be specific applications where it will be opportune to consider more axes.

Each level of autonomy in Table 2 will correspond to certain capabilities in the three dimensions illustrated in Fig. 6. It is easy to imagine that a robot at LoA 1 will have limited capabilities in all the three dimensions, while a robot at LoA 6 will have high capabilities in all dimensions. It is not so straightforward to imagine how intermediate LoAs will correspond to capabilities in the three dimensions. In fact, to the same intermediate LoA it may correspond different capabilities depending on the specific application and the current priorities: for example, the R&D plans for a specific underwater intervention drone may move towards higher LoAs by prioritizing first the increase of capabilities within machine operation/automation and only at a later stage the data integration/deliberation capabilities.

## 5 Conclusions

This paper highlighted several important aspects defining autonomous mobile robots for asset owners in the energy industry. To realize the large innovation opportunities within robotics and digital technologies, the metric for autonomy needs to account for these aspects and to reflect the business drivers in the industry. Therefore, a multidimensional measure of autonomy is recommended.

However, there is still a way to go before arriving to suitable autonomy requirements and specifications for the engineering of solutions for the energy industry. This is a challenge to be addressed together by all actors in the market. There are also opportunities to leverage the learning and experience from other industries.

There are many related topics that have not been addressed in this paper, which are as well important for successful autonomous robot applications. These include: safe failure policies for critical operations; autonomous robot system architecture for industry applications; communication infrastructure supporting remote control, edge and cloud computing; collaborative robots performing complex tasks; system security; standardization and integration of robotic systems from different vendors.

## References

1. Chen, H., Stavinoha, S., Walker, M., Zhang, B., Fuhlbrigge, T.: Opportunities and challenges of robotics and automation in offshore oil and gas industry. Intell. Control Autom. **5**, 136–145 (2014)
2. Shukla, A., Karki, H.: A review of robotics in onshore oil-gas industry. In: International Conference of Mechatronics and Automation, pp. 1153–1160 (2013)
3. Norvig, P., Russell, S.J.: Artificial Intelligence: A Modern Approach, 3rd edn. Prentice Hall, Upper Saddle River (2018)
4. Rich, E., Knight, K.: Artificial Intelligence. McGraw-Hill, New York (1991)

5. Kurzweil, R.: The Age of Intelligent Machines. MIT Press, Cambridge (1990)
6. Schultz, M.A., Goodrich, A.C.: Human-robot interaction: a survey. Found. Trends Hum. Comput. Interact. **1**(3), 203–275 (2007)
7. Vagia, M., Transeth, A.A., Fjerdingen, S.A.: A literature review on the levels of automation during the years. What are the different taxonomies that have been proposed? Appl. Ergon. **53**, 190–202 (2015)
8. SAE International: Taxonomy and Definitions for Terms Related to Driving Automation Systems for On-Road Motor Vehicles (2018)
9. Norwegian Forum for Autonomous Ships (NFAS): Definitions for Autonomous Merchant Ships (2017)
10. Sheridan, T.B., Verplank, W.L.: Human and Computer Control for Undersea Teleoperators. Massachusetts Institute of Technology, Man-Machine Systems Laboratory (1978)
11. Proud, R.W., Hart, J.J., Mrozinski, R.B.: Methods for determining the level of autonomy to design into a human spaceflight vehicle: a function specific approach, NASA (2005)
12. National Institute of Standards and Technology (NIST): Autonomy Levels for Unmanned Systems (ALFUS) framework v2.0, NIST Special Publication 1011-I-2.0 (2008)
13. Riley, V.: A general model of mixed-initiative human-machine systems. In: 33rd Annual Meeting of the Human Factors Society, vol. 33, no. 2, pp. 124–128 (1989)
14. Ingrand, F., Ghallab, M.: Deliberation for autonomous robots: a survey. Artif. Intell. **247**, 10–44 (2017)

# Multimodal 3D Object Detection
# from Simulated Pretraining

Åsmund Brekke⬡, Fredrik Vatsendvik^(✉)⬡, and Frank Lindseth⬡

Norwegian University of Science and Technology, Trondheim, Norway
{aasmunhb,fredrva}@stud.ntnu.no, frankl@ntnu.no

**Abstract.** The need for simulated data in autonomous driving applications has become increasingly important, both for validation of pretrained models and for training new models. In order for these models to generalize to real-world applications, it is critical that the underlying dataset contains a variety of driving scenarios and that simulated sensor readings closely mimics real-world sensors. We present the Carla Automated Dataset Extraction Tool (CADET), a novel tool for generating training data from the CARLA simulator to be used in autonomous driving research. The tool is able to export high-quality, synchronized LIDAR and camera data with object annotations, and offers configuration to accurately reflect a real-life sensor array. Furthermore, we use this tool to generate a dataset consisting of 10 000 samples and use this dataset in order to train the 3D object detection network AVOD-FPN, with finetuning on the KITTI dataset in order to evaluate the potential for effective pretraining. We also present two novel LIDAR feature map configurations in Bird's Eye View for use with AVOD-FPN that can be easily modified. These configurations are tested on the KITTI and CADET datasets in order to evaluate their performance as well as the usability of the simulated dataset for pretraining. Although insufficient to fully replace the use of real world data, and generally not able to exceed the performance of systems fully trained on real data, our results indicate that simulated data can considerably reduce the amount of training on real data required to achieve satisfactory levels of accuracy.

**Keywords:** Autonomous driving · Simulated data · 3D object detection · CARLA · KITTI · AVOD-FPN · LIDAR · Sensor fusion

## 1 Introduction

Machine learning models are becoming increasingly complex, with deeper architectures and a rapid increase in the number of parameters. The expressive power of such models allow for more possibilities than ever before, but require large amounts of labeled data to properly train. Labeling of data in the autonomous driving domain requires extensive amounts of manual labour, either in the form of actively producing annotations such as class labels, bounding boxes and semantic segmentation by hand, or by supervising and adjusting automated generation of these using a pretrained ensemble of models from previously labeled

© Springer Nature Switzerland AG 2019
K. Bach and M. Ruocco (Eds.): NAIS 2019, CCIS 1056, pp. 102–113, 2019.
https://doi.org/10.1007/978-3-030-35664-4_10

data. For the use of modern sensors such as LIDAR, not many sizable labeled datasets exists, and those that do generally offer little variation in terms of environments or weather conditions to properly allow for generalization to real world conditions. Popular datasets such as KITTI [2] offers a large array of sensors, but with largely unchanging weather conditions and lighting, while the larger and more diverse BDD100K [3] dataset does not include multimodal sensor data, only offering camera and GPS/IMU. The possibility of new sensors being introduced that greatly impact autonomous driving also carry the risk of invalidating the use of existing datasets for training state-of-the-art solutions.

## 1.1 Simulated Data for Autonomous Driving

With the advances in recent years in the field of computer graphics, both in terms of photorealism and accelerated computation, simulation has been a vital method of validating autonomous models in unseen environments due to the efficiency of generating different scenarios [13]. More recently there has been added interest in the use of modern simulators for also generating the data used to train models for autonomous vehicles, both for perception and end-to-end reinforcement learning [10–12]. There are several advantages in generating training data through simulation. Large datasets, with diverse conditions can be quickly generated provided enough computational resources, while labeling can be fully automated with little need for supervision. Specific, difficult scenarios can be more easily constructed and advanced sensors can be added provided they have been accurately modeled. Systems such as the NVIDIA Drive Constellation [5] are pushing the boundaries for photorealistic simulation for autonomous driving using clusters of powerful NVIDIA GPUs, but is currently only available to automakers, startups and selected research institutions using NVIDIAs Drive Pegasus AI car computer, and only offers validation of models, not data generation for training. However, open source solutions based on state-of-the-art game engines such as Unreal Engine 4 and Unity, are currently in active development and offer a range of features enabling anyone to generate high quality simulations for autonomous driving. Notable examples include CARLA [1] and AirSim [4], the former of which was used for this research.

## 2   Simulation Toolkit

In order to facilitate the training and validation of machine learning models for autonomous driving using simulated data, the authors introduce the Carla Automated Dataset Extraction Tool (CADET) [8], an open-source tool for generating labeled data for autonomous driving models, compatible with Carla 0.8. The tool supports various functionality including LIDAR to camera projection (Fig. 1), generation of 2D and 3D bounding box labels for cars and pedestrians (Fig. 2), detection of partially occluded objects (Fig. 3), and generation of sensor data including LIDAR, camera and ground plane estimation, as well as sensor calibration matrices. All labels and calibration matrices are stored in the data format defined by Geiger et al. [2], which makes it compatible with a number of existing models for object detection and segmentation. As a varied dataset is crucial for a machine learning model to generalize from a simulated environment to real-life scenarios, the data generation tool includes a number of measures to ensure variety. Most importantly, the tool resets the environment after a fixed number of samples generated. Here, a sample is defined as the tuple containing a reading from each sensor, corresponding ground truth labels and calibration data. Resetting the environment entails randomization of vehicle models, spawn positions, weather conditions and maps, and ensures a uniform distribution of weather types, agent models for both pedestrians and cars and starting positions of all vehicles. The LIDAR and camera sensors are positioned identically and synchronized such that a full LIDAR rotation exists for each image[1]. The raw sensor data is projected to a unified coordinate system used in Unreal Engine 4 before determining visible objects in the scene, and projecting to the relative coordinate spaces used in KITTI. As the initial LIDAR configuration in CARLA ignores the pitch and roll of the vehicle it is attached to, additional transformations are applied after projection such that the sensor data is properly aligned. One challenge when generating object labels is determining the visible objects in the current scene. In order to detect occluded objects, the CARLA *depth map* is utilized. A vertex is defined as occluded if the value of one of its neighbouring pixels in the depth map is closer than the vertex distance to the camera. An object is defined as occluded if at least four out of its eight bounding box vertices are occluded. This occlusion detection performs satisfactory and much faster than tracing the whole object, even when objects are localized behind see-through objects such as chain-link fences, shown in Fig. 3. A more robust occlusion detection can be performed by using the semantic segmentation of the scene, but this is not implemented as of yet.

**Fig. 1.** LIDAR point cloud projected to image space. The color of each LIDAR point is determined by its depth value (Color figure online).

---

[1] Note that this only implies an approximate correspondance between points from the camera and LIDAR sensors.

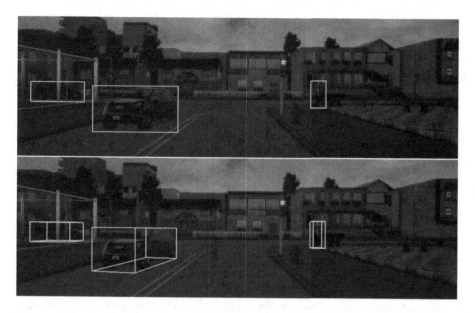

**Fig. 2.** 2D (top) and 3D (bottom) bounding boxes as generated by CADET. Class labels are omitted.

**Fig. 3.** Occluded vertices behind a chain fence. Note that both cars are visible, and thus have a bounding box drawn around them. Occluded and visible vertices are drawn with red and green, respectively (Color figure online).

## 3   Generated Dataset

Using CADET we generate the CADET dataset, consisting of 10 000 samples. In total, there are 13989 cars and 4895 pedestrians in the dataset, averaging about 1.9 labeled objects per image. The dataset contains 2D and 3D bounding box annotations of the classes Car and Pedestrian, and contains both LIDAR and camera sensor data, as well as ground plane estimation and generation of sensor calibration matrices. The environment is generated from two maps,

namely *Town01* and *Town02* in the CARLA simulator, which are both subur-
ban environments. The distribution of objects in each image is shown in Fig. 8.
In comparison with the KITTI dataset, the CADET dataset has less cars and
pedestrians per image, which is mostly due to city-environment of KITTI, where
cars are frequently parked at the side of the road and pedestrians are present in
a higher degree. The orientation of each labeled object is shown in Fig. 9. We
observe that the distribution of orientation have a sharp multimodal distribution
with three peaks, namely for objects seen from the front, behind or sideways.
Note that the pedestrians in the dataset generally have a smaller bounding box
than cars, shown in Fig. 7, making them harder to detect.

## 4    Training on Simulated Data

In order to evaluate the use of the simulated CADET dataset, as well experiment with LIDAR feature map representations, several configurations were used
of the AVOD-FPN [6] architecture for 3D object detection using camera and
LIDAR point cloud. The AVOD-FPN source code has been altered to allow for
customized configurations by specifying the features wanted for two groups, slice
maps and cloud maps. Slice maps refer to feature maps taken from each vertical
slice the point cloud is split into, as specified in the configuration files, while the
cloud maps consider the whole point cloud. Following the approach described
in [6], two networks were used for detecting cars and pedestrians separately,
repeating the process for each configuration. As multiclass detection might also
produce more unstable results when evaluating per class, this was considered
the better option. All models used a feature pyramid network to extract features from images and LIDAR, with early fusion of the extracted camera and
LIDAR features. Training data is augmented using flipping and jitter, with the
only differences between models of the same class being the respective representations of LIDAR feature maps in Bird's Eye View (BEV) as described in
Sect. 4.1. All configurations used are available in the source code [9].

### 4.1    Model Configurations

AVOD-FPN uses a simplified feature extractor based on the VGG-16 architecture [14] to produce feature maps from camera view as well as LIDAR projected
to BEV, allowing the LIDAR to be processed by a Convolutional Neural Network
(CNN) designed for 2D images. These separate feature maps are fused together
using trainable weights, allowing the model to learn how to best combine multimodal information. In addition to what will be referred to as the default BEV
configuration, as proposed in [6], two additional novel configurations are proposed for which experimental results either show faster inference with similar
accuracy, or better accuracy with similar inference speed. In all cases the BEV
is discretized horizontally into cells at a resolution of 0.1m. The default configuration creates 5 equally sized vertical slices within a specified height range,
taking the highest point in each cell normalized by the slice height. A separate

image for the density of the entire point cloud is generated from the number of points $N$ in each cell following Eq. 1, as used in [6] and [7], though normalized by $log(64)$ in the latter. We propose a simplified structure, taking the global maximum height, minimum height and density of each cell over the entire point cloud, avoiding the use of slices and halving the amount of BEV maps. We argue that this is sufficient to determine which points belong to large objects and which are outliers, and that it sufficiently defines box dimensions. For classes that occupy less space, we argue that taking three slices vertically using the maximum height and density for each slice can perform better with less susceptibility to noise, as the network could potentially learn to distinguish whether the maximum height value of a slice belongs to the object or not depending on the slice density. All configurations are visualized in Figs. 4, 5 and 6.

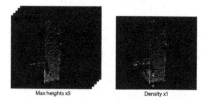

**Fig. 4.** Visualization of default BEV configuration, taking the maximum height within 5 vertical slices as well as the density of the full point cloud.

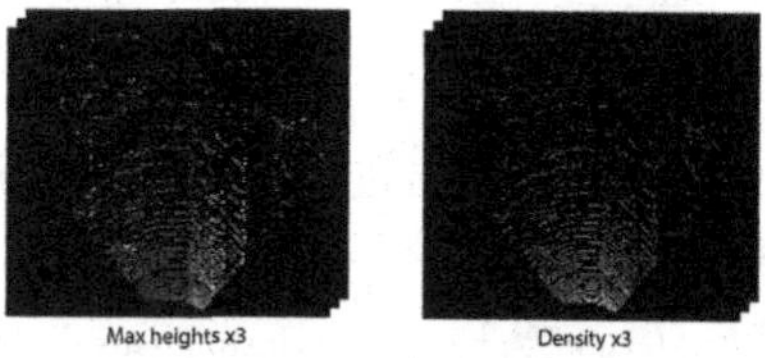

**Fig. 5.** Visualization of first custom BEV configuration, taking the maximum height and density within 3 vertical slices.

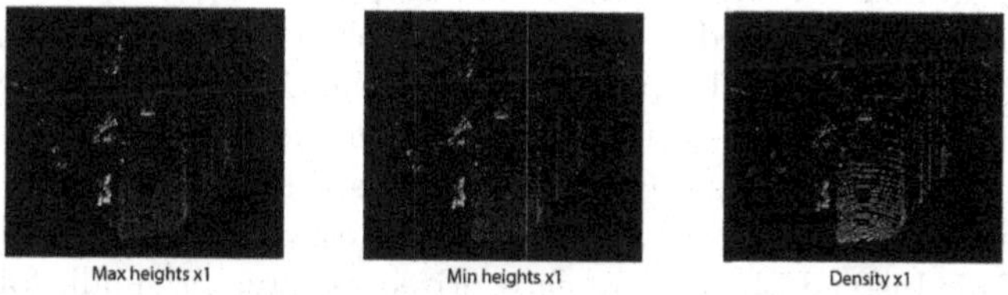

**Fig. 6.** Visualization of second custom BEV configuration, taking the maximum height, minimum height and density of the full point cloud.

$$min(1.0, \frac{log(N+1)}{log(16)})  \tag{1}$$

## 4.2  Results

In order to gather qualitative results each model trained for a total of 120k steps on the respective datasets, with a batch size of 1, as described in [6]. Checkpoints were stored at every 2k steps, of which the last 20 were selected for evaluation.

Tables 1 and 2 show generated results on the KITTI dataset, for the Car and Pedestrian classes respectively, selecting the best performing checkpoint for each of the 3 BEV configurations. To measure inference speed, each model performs inference on the first 2000 images of the validation set, with learning deactivated, using a NVIDIA GTX 1080 graphics card. The mean inference time is rounded up to the nearest millisecond and presented in the tables.

**Table 1.** KITTI-trained model evaluated on the KITTI dataset for the Car class

| Method | Runtime (ms) | $AP_{3D}(\%)$ | | | $AP_{BEV}(\%)$ | | |
|---|---|---|---|---|---|---|---|
| | | Easy | Moderate | Hard | Easy | Moderate | Hard |
| Default | 119 | **83.46** | 73.94 | 67.81 | 89.37 | 86.44 | 78.64 |
| Max*3, Density*3 | 120 | 83.16 | **73.97** | **67.98** | **89.84** | **86.62** | **79.85** |
| Max, Min, Density | **114** | 82.98 | 73.92 | 67.84 | 89.62 | 86.61 | 79.68 |

**Table 2.** KITTI-trained model evaluated on the KITTI dataset for the Pedestrian class

| Method | Runtime (ms) | $AP_{3D}(\%)$ | | | $AP_{BEV}(\%)$ | | |
|---|---|---|---|---|---|---|---|
| | | Easy | Moderate | Hard | Easy | Moderate | Hard |
| Default | 122 | 41.05 | 37.00 | 32.00 | 44.12 | 39.54 | 38.11 |
| Max*3, Density*3 | 122 | **45.61** | **42.66** | **38.06** | **49.16** | **45.99** | **44.53** |
| Max, Min, Density | **117** | 27.85 | 27.17 | 24.54 | 33.39 | 33.10 | 29.78 |

Following evaluation on the KITTI dataset, all configurations were trained from scratch on the generated CADET dataset following the exact same process. Results from evaluation on the validation set of the CADET dataset can be seen in Tables 3 and 4. Note that as dynamic occlusion and truncation measurements are not included in the dataset (these are only used for post training evaluation in KITTI), evaluation does not follow the regular easy, moderate, hard categories used in KITTI. Instead objects are categorized as large or small, following the minimum height requirements for the bounding boxes of 40 pixels for easy and 25 pixels for moderate and hard. These models were additionally evaluated directly on the KITTI validation set, with results summarized in Tables 5 and 6.

**Table 3.** CADET-trained model evaluated on the CADET dataset for the Car class

| Method | $AP_{3D}(\%)$ | | $AP_{BEV}(\%)$ | |
|---|---|---|---|---|
| | Large | Small | Large | Small |
| Default | 70.86 | 69.37 | **80.13** | **71.32** |
| Max*3, Density*3 | **70.96** | **69.59** | 79.81 | 71.28 |
| Max, Min, Density | 68.79 | 60.87 | 78.75 | 70.72 |

**Table 4.** CADET-trained model evaluated on the CADET dataset for the Pedestrian class

| Method | $AP_{3D}(\%)$ | | $AP_{BEV}(\%)$ | |
|---|---|---|---|---|
| | Large | Small | Large | Small |
| Default | 75.43 | **73.89** | 75.43 | **73.91** |
| Max*3, Density*3 | **76.13** | 72.99 | **80.24** | 73.41 |
| Max, Min, Density | 75.49 | 71.82 | 79.73 | 72.37 |

**Table 5.** CADET-trained model evaluated on the KITTI dataset for the Car class

| Method | $AP_{3D}(\%)$ | | | $AP_{BEV}(\%)$ | | |
|---|---|---|---|---|---|---|
| | Easy | Moderate | Hard | Easy | Moderate | Hard |
| Default | 29.85 | 20.29 | 18.40 | 50.58 | 37.81 | 30.77 |
| Max*3, Density*3 | **35.85** | **29.40** | **24.99** | **57.32** | **49.63** | **43.25** |
| Max, Min, Density | 30.34 | 24.28 | 20.25 | 45.22 | 37.56 | 31.17 |

**Table 6.** CADET-trained model evaluated on the KITTI dataset for the Pedestrian class

| Method | $AP_{3D}(\%)$ | | | $AP_{BEV}(\%)$ | | |
|---|---|---|---|---|---|---|
| | Easy | Moderate | Hard | Easy | Moderate | Hard |
| Default | **9.09** | **9.09** | **9.09** | 9.38 | **9.33** | **9.38** |
| Max*3, Density*3 | 2.27 | 2.27 | 2.27 | 2.27 | 2.27 | 2.27 |
| Max, Min, Density | **9.09** | **9.09** | **9.09** | **9.78** | 9.09 | 9.09 |

**Table 7.** CADET-trained model, fine-tuned and evaluated on the KITTI dataset for the Car class

| Method | $AP_{3D}(\%)$ | | | $AP_{BEV}(\%)$ | | |
|---|---|---|---|---|---|---|
| | Easy | Moderate | Hard | Easy | Moderate | Hard |
| Default | **83.84** | 68.67 | **67.40** | **89.41** | 79.77 | **78.86** |
| Max*3, Density*3 | 76.85 | **72.44** | 66.55 | 88.20 | **85.18** | 78.71 |
| Max, Min, Density | 81.00 | 66.95 | 65.88 | 88.76 | 79.36 | 78.41 |

The CADET-trained models were subsequently restored from their check-points at step 90k and modified for further training on the KITTI dataset. Training was resumed until step 150k, meaning the models received 60k steps of training on the KITTI training set as opposed to 120k originally. Other than increasing the amount of steps and switching the target datasets,

**Table 8.** CADET-trained model, fine-tuned and evaluated on the KITTI dataset for the Pedestrian class

| Method | $AP_{3D}(\%)$ | | | $AP_{BEV}(\%)$ | | |
|---|---|---|---|---|---|---|
| | Easy | Moderate | Hard | Easy | Moderate | Hard |
| Default | **40.26** | **38.55** | 33.93 | **46.96** | **44.80** | **40.73** |
| Max*3, Density*3 | 39.19 | 38.02 | **34.15** | 46.14 | 43.54 | 40.44 |
| Max, Min, Density | 37.32 | 34.34 | 32.60 | 45.71 | 42.43 | 37.62 |

the configuration files were not altered from when training on the CADET dataset. Tables 7 and 8 show results from the top performing checkpoint of each model.

# 5   Discussion

For the fully KITTI-trained models, results on the Car class are very similar for all configurations, where the largest loss in amounts to only 0.5% 3D AP on the easy category from the default configuration to our configuration using half as many layers in the BEV map. Larger differences are apparent for the Pedestrian class, where 3 layers is not sufficient to compete with the default configuration. However, the use of 3 slices of maximum heights and density, totalling 6 layers as with the default configuration, shows noticeably better results across the board suggesting a more robust behaviour.

Evaluation of the CADET-trained models on the CADET validation set shows similar relative performance between the models, however with the simpler custom configuration showing a dip in accuracy for the moderate category on the Car class. With regards to pedestrians, differences are much smaller than what could have been expected. Also considering the unremarkable and rather inconsistent performance on the Pedestrian class of the KITTI dataset, we can likely accredit this to overly simplified representation of the physical collision of pedestrians visible in the simulated LIDAR point cloud. The CADET-trained models do perform better on the Car class however, suggesting better and more consistent generalization for this task.

The fine-tuned models show performance on the Car class mostly similar to the fully KITTI-trained models, however with each model showing a noticeable drop in performance on either the easy or moderate category. Results on the Pedestrian class are a bit more interesting. The default configuration sees a slight increase in accuracy on the moderate and hard category, with a slight decrease for easy. The max/density configuration sees a significant decrease in performance on all categories, where as the less complex max/min/density configuration, although still being the weakest performer, sees a significant increase in performance compared to when only trained on the KITTI dataset. The reason for the rather inconsistent results when compared to the KITTI-trained models are not thoroughly investigated, but can in part be due to somewhat unstable

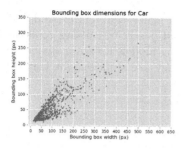
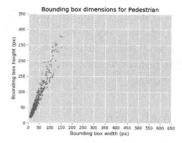

**Fig. 7.** Dimension of 2D bounding boxes for the classes in the CADET dataset.

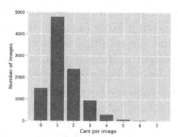
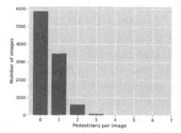

**Fig. 8.** Number of annotations for each class per image in the CADET dataset.

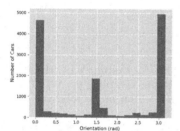
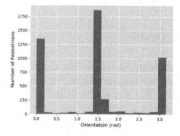

**Fig. 9.** Distribution of orientation per class in the CADET dataset.

gradients not producing fully reliable results. The CARLA generated LIDAR point cloud does not feature accurate geometry due to simplified collision of all dynamic objects. As such the different capabilities of the configurations may not be exploited during the pretraining on the CADET dataset, impacting overall results. The simplest configuration significantly closing the gap on the Pedestrian class may be a testament to this, as the simplified pedestrian representation is more easily recognizable.

While results from simulated and partly simulated training do not generally exceed the performance of direct training on the dataset, there is a clear indication that the use of simulated data can achieve closely matched performance with less training on actual data. The ease of generation and expandabililty in terms of sensors, scenarios, environments and conditions makes tools such as CADET very useful for training and evaluating models for autonomous driving, although improvements are needed before they are sufficient for training real world solutions.

## 6   Conclusion

In recent years, the use of synthetic data for training machine learning models has gained in popularity due to the costs associated with gathering real-life data. This is especially true with regards to autonomous driving because of the strict demand of generalizability to a diverse number of driving scenarios. In this study, we have described CADET - a tool for generating large amounts of training data for perception in autonomous driving, and the resulting dataset. We have demonstrated that this dataset, while not sufficient to directly train systems for use in the real world, is useful in lowering the amount of real-life data required to train machine learning models to reasonably high levels of accuracy. We have also suggested and evaluated two novel BEV representations, easily configurable before training, with potential for better detection of smaller objects and reduced complexity for detection of larger objects respectively. The CADET toolkit, while still requiring improved physical models in LIDAR modelling, is currently able to generate datasets for training and validation of virtually any model designed for the KITTI object detection task.

## References

1. Dosovitskiy, A., Ros, G., Codevilla, F., Lopez, A., Koltun, V.: CARLA: an open urban driving simulator. In: Conference on Robot Learning, pp. 1–16 (2017)
2. Geiger, A., Lenz, P., Stiller, C., Urtasun, R.: Vision meets robotics: the KITTI dataset. Int. J. Robot. Res. **32**, 1231–1237 (2013)
3. Yu, F., et al.: BDD100K: A diverse driving video database with scalable annotation tooling. arXiv preprint arXiv:1805.04687 (2018)
4. Shah, S., Dey, D., Lovett, C., Kapoor, A.: AirSim: high-fidelity visual and physical simulation for autonomous vehicles. In: Hutter, M., Siegwart, R. (eds.) Field and Service Robotics. SPAR, vol. 5, pp. 621–635. Springer, Cham (2018). https://doi.org/10.1007/978-3-319-67361-5_40
5. NVIDIA Drive Constellation Homepage (2019). https://www.nvidia.com/en-us/self-driving-cars/drive-constellation. Accessed 8 Apr 2019
6. Ku, J., Mozifian, M., Lee, J., Harakeh, A., Waslander, S.L.: Joint 3D proposal generation and object detection from view aggregation. In: 2018 IEEE/RSJ International Conference on Intelligent Robots and Systems (IROS), pp. 1–8. IEEE (2018)
7. Chen, X., Ma, H., Wan, J., Li, B., Xia, T.: Multi-view 3D object detection network for autonomous driving. In: Proceedings of the IEEE Conference on Computer Vision and Pattern Recognition, pp. 1907–1915 (2017)
8. Brekke, Å., Vatsendvik, F.: CARLA data export tool (2019). https://github.com/Ozzyz/carla-data-export/

9. Modified AVOD architecture (2019). https://github.com/Fredrik00/avod. Accessed 8 Apr 2019
10. Kiran, B.R., Roldão, L., Irastorza, B., Verastegui, R., Süss, S., Yogamani, S., Talpaert, V., Lepoutre, A., Trehard, G.: Real-time dynamic object detection for autonomous driving using prior 3D-maps. In: Leal-Taixé, L., Roth, S. (eds.) ECCV 2018. LNCS, vol. 11133, pp. 567–582. Springer, Cham (2019). https://doi.org/10.1007/978-3-030-11021-5_35
11. Codevilla, F., et al.: End-to-end driving via conditional imitation learning. In: 2018 IEEE International Conference on Robotics and Automation (ICRA), pp. 1–9. IEEE (2018)
12. Gaidon, A., Lopez, A., Perronnin, F.: The reasonable effectiveness of synthetic visual data. Int. J. Comput. Vision **126**(9), 899–901 (2018)
13. Schöner, H.P.: Simulation in development and testing of autonomous vehicles. In: Bargende, M., Reuss, H.C., Wiedemann, J. (eds.) Internationales Stuttgarter Symposium. P, pp. 1083–1095. Springer, Wiesbaden (2018). https://doi.org/10.1007/978-3-658-21194-3_82
14. Simonyan, K., Zisserman, A.: Very deep convolutional networks for large-scale image recognition. arXiv preprint arXiv:1409.1556 (2014)

# A Comparative Analysis of Feature Selection Methods for Biomarker Discovery in Study of Toxicant-Treated Atlantic Cod (*Gadus Morhua*) Liver

Xiaokang Zhang and Inge Jonassen$^{(\boxtimes)}$

Computational Biology Unit, Department of Informatics,
University of Bergen, Bergen, Norway
{xiaokang.zhang,inge.jonassen}@uib.no
https://www.cbu.uib.no/jonassen/

**Abstract.** Univariate and multivariate feature selection methods can be used for biomarker discovery in analysis of toxicant exposure. Among the univariate methods, differential expression analysis (DEA) is often applied for its simplicity and interpretability. A characteristic of methods for DEA is that they treat genes individually, disregarding the correlation that exists between them. On the other hand, some multivariate feature selection methods are proposed for biomarker discovery. Provided with various biomarker discovery methods, how to choose the most suitable method for a specific dataset becomes a problem. In this paper, we present a framework for comparison of potential biomarker discovery methods: three methods that stem from different theories are compared by how stable they are and how well they can improve the classification accuracy. The three methods we have considered are: Significance Analysis of Microarrays (SAM) which identifies the differentially expressed genes; minimum Redundancy Maximum Relevance (mRMR) based on information theory; and Characteristic Direction (GeoDE) inspired by a graphical perspective. Tested on the gene expression data from two experiments exposing the cod fish to two different toxicants (MeHg and PCB 153), different methods stand out in different cases, so a decision upon the most suitable method should be made based on the dataset under study and the research interest.

**Keywords:** Feature selection · Stability · Classification · Biomarker discovery

## 1 Introduction

Atlantic cod (*Gadus morhua*) is one of the most important commercial fish species in Norway [1], forming the basis for fisheries, trade, and, historically, civilization. Unfortunately, cod is increasingly susceptible to marine pollution from petroleum activities [2,3]. Atlantic cod is commonly used as an indicator species in marine environmental monitoring programs, and a useful model organism to investigate

© Springer Nature Switzerland AG 2019
K. Bach and M. Ruocco (Eds.): NAIS 2019, CCIS 1056, pp. 114–123, 2019.
https://doi.org/10.1007/978-3-030-35664-4_11

the effect of toxicants [4–6]. Finding the best set of biomarkers for Atlantic cod exposed to toxicants is of high research and commercial value. Biomarkers can for example be defined based on the expression level of a set of genes or proteins. Biomarker discovery is an essential part in study of toxicant exposure, and many methods have been proposed to find biomarkers [7]. However, a remaining question is, provided with numbers of biomarker discovery methods, which method is the most suitable one for a particular dataset. This paper provides a framework to compare potential biomarker discovery methods and to give researchers a better basis for choosing which one to use for the task at hand.

In the context of statistics and machine learning, biomarker discovery corresponds to a feature selection problem, where the purpose is to identify the most distinguishing features, for example, distinguishing normal and toxicant-treated cod livers. The task of feature selection is to identify, from a wide range of features, those that are best suited for classification.

The strategies of feature selection methods can be divided into two categories [7]:

1. Classical univariate statistical methods, where the features are considered as independent from each other. Genes that are differentially expressed are regarded as biomarkers.
2. Multivariate methods, which take the interaction between features into consideration when selecting the important features allowing to distinguish samples coming from different groups.

The classical univariate methods try to find the features having significantly different values between the different groups, e.g. control group and treated group. One of the most popular and basic methods is Student's t-test [8]. Some similar research also adopted Analysis of Variance (ANOVA) and Significance Analysis of Microarrays (SAM) to find the differential expressed genes [9–13]. A main drawback of such approaches is that they rest on the assumption that all the genes or proteins are independent from each other, which is clearly not true, since both genes and proteins are part of a biological system where they interact with each other [14,15].

On the other hand, multivariate methods will take the interaction among features into consideration, reflecting that the features are acting in groups. Many feature selection and machine learning methods try to find the features most correlated with the class labels and take the interaction among features into consideration at the same time.

Feature selection methods are often divided into three categories: filter methods which focus on the relation between feature values and class labels; wrapper methods which use an objective function (can be the classification accuracy of the classifier) to evaluate features; and embedded methods where the classifier selects the features automatically [16]. The latter two are both classifier-dependent, and filter methods are more like a one-way decision without feedback from prediction accuracy. In order to find a more general feature selection method, which does not only work well with one specific classifier, we will only focus on the filter methods.

In toxicant exposure study, or more generally, in the context of biology, very often, researchers are faced with the high-dimension-small-sample-size issue, since it is hard and expensive to get a high number of samples (it is often around 10 or even lower), but the number of features (genes or proteins) is usually very high (over one thousand). In such cases, two problems are difficult to avoid: finding a reliable feature subset, as in this case the possibility of chance correlation is quite high; assuring that the selected features are true biomarkers. The true biomarkers should be data-independent, meaning that a small change in the samples should not lead to a large change in the selected features, which requires the feature selection method to be stable. Besides of that, they should also be qualified to be treated as the representatives of the whole feature list and should therefore be able to improve a classifier's prediction accuracy while classifying samples from different biological conditions. Therefore, we will compare the feature selection methods based on two aspects of their performance: stability to find a reliable feature subset and ability to improve a classifier's prediction accuracy.

To make the work reproducible, all the data sets and source codes are publicly available at https://github.com/zhxiaokang/FScompare.

## 2   Methods

### 2.1   Data Sets

Two datasets from study of toxicant-treated Atlantic cod liver are used here. One is from the study of the hepatic proteome of MeHg-exposed Atlantic cod, where there are 10 samples in control group, 9 samples in low-dose treated group (0.5 mg/kg Body Weight MeHg), and 9 samples in high-dose treated group (2 mg/kg BW MeHg). The abundances of 1143 proteins were measured after the samples were exposed in vivo to MeHg for two weeks [12]. The other study is from the quantitative proteomics analysis of Atlantic cod livers treated with PCB 153 of various doses of PCB 153 (0, 0.5, 2 and 8 mg/kg BW PCB 153) for two weeks. There are 10 samples in each control group, low-dose treated group, medium-dose treated group, and high-dose treated group. Then 1272 liver proteins are quantified [13].

### 2.2   Principle of Method and Notations

Consider a set of $m$ samples $\{x_i, y_i\}$ ($i = 1, 2, \ldots m$). Each sample has $n$ input variables $x_{i,j}$ ($j = 1, 2, \ldots n$) and one output variable $y_i$. From the original feature set $F$, a feature selection method will select a subset $S$ of $k$ variables.

Suppose that there are $P$ feature selection methods to be compared. Using Leave-One-Out Cross-Validation (LOOCV), $m$ feature subsets will be generated for each pre-defined value of $k$. The stability of each feature selection method $Stab_{p,k}$ ($p = 1, 2, \ldots P$) can be calculated based on those $m$ subsets.

To test their ability to improve a classifier's prediction accuracy, the generated feature subsets will then be applied to train a classifier and the prediction accuracy of the corresponding classifier will also be measured. Area Under the Curve (AUC) is used to measure the classifier's prediction accuracy [17]. If tested on $Q$ classifiers, the prediction accuracy of each classifier can be calculated $AUC_{p,q,k}$ ($q = 1, 2, ...Q$). Considering both matrices $Stab$ and $AUC$, a general evaluation of each feature selection method can finally be achieved so that researchers can choose a proper method for their data.

But the stability does not necessarily agree with the prediction accuracy: the most stable feature selection method may not achieve the highest prediction accuracy. Then the researchers need to balance between these two measures according to their preference and the needs of the project.

## 2.3  Feature Selection Methods

Some representatives of those two strategies (univariate and multivariate) are compared. For the univariate methods, SAM is applied here, since it was used in the literature from where our data comes. SAM was designed to identify genes with significantly differential expression in microarray experiments. For the multivariate methods, we utilize minimum Redundancy Maximum Relevance (mRMR) [18] and Characteristic Direction from a geometrical aspect (GeoDE) [19]. mRMR is based on information theory. It tries to find out the feature subset in which the redundancy among the features are minimized and the relevance of features and the targeted classes are maximized. GeoDE uses linear discriminant analysis to define a separating hyperplane and the orientation of the hyperplane is used to identify the differentially expressed genes.

Those methods are selected for our comparison because they are based on different theories so that our results are more likely to be valid in general, and they are all widely used biomarker discovery methods. So $P$ equals 3 in this case, but researchers can always compare as many feature selection methods as they want.

## 2.4  Performance Measurement

Performance of feature selection methods is measured by two factors: stability and accuracy.

Many measures of stability have been proposed. Nogueira et al. studied 15 different measures proposed between 2002 and 2018 and also proposed their novel measure [20]. In our case where the purpose is to compare the stability of different feature selection methods, the absolute values of stability are not that important as long as they are comparable for different methods under the same settings. In each round of comparison, the number of selected features $k$ is a constant, so the stability measure does not need to be able to cope with various numbers of features. LOOCV will generate more than two feature sets based on which the stability is calculated, so the measures which are defined for a pair of feature sets are not proper choices. Considering the measures that satisfy all the requirements, we chose StabPerf [21] for its simplicity and interpretability. The stability is defined as:

$$Stab_{p,k} = \frac{\sum_{f \in F}(freq(f)/m)}{|F|} \tag{1}$$

Where $Stab_{p,k}$ is the stability of a given feature selection method $p$ with a predefined $k$; $m$ is the number of feature subsets analyzed; $F$ is the set of features that appear in at least one of the $m$ subsets and $|F|$ indicates the cardinality of $F$; $freq(f)$ is the frequency of feature $f \in F$ that appears in those $m$ subsets.

To test the ability to improve a classifier's prediction accuracy, four popular classification methods are utilized here: Random Forest (RF) [22], Support Vector Machine (SVM) [23], and extended two-class logistic regression (RIDGE and LASSO are applied) [24].

## 2.5   Cross-Validation Approach

We characterize our problem as a two-class classification problem: the control group versus the treated group. In the process of classification, we need to divide the samples into training set and testing set. But since the number of samples is quite limited, we apply the strategy of LOOCV, which means that in every training-prediction process, we leave one sample out as testing set, and use the other samples as training set to search for the most important features and to train a classifier. With $m$ samples, we will use the $i^{th}$ sample to test the prediction accuracy of the classifier trained from the other $m - 1$ samples. The average of performance observed over all $m$ predictions will be regarded as the estimate of the performance of the model trained over the whole sample set. To avoid overfitting or an overly optimistic estimate, it should be noted that the feature selection and training of classifiers are only limited to the training set, to avoid the information from the testing set leaking into the model training procedure [25]. That makes the size of testing set decided by the number of samples in one classification problem, e.g. 19 in MeHg's high-dose case. Moreover, 19 samples indicate 19 rounds of feature selection and prediction, resulting in 19 selected feature subsets and 19 * 4 classifiers. Therefore, if a feature selection method is stable enough, there should be a big overlap among these 19 selected feature subsets; at best the feature subsets would be identical. And if the selected features are true biomarkers, the resulting 76 classifiers should yield high prediction accuracies.

To make our comparison more stable, avoiding the accidental findings, and to analyze the characteristic of the feature selection methods, we repeat the above process with different numbers of selected features (ranging from 40 to 400 with a step of 40, but also including 12 and 24 to look into more details with small numbers of selected features where the output varies a lot).

Tukey's Honestly Significant Difference Test (Tukey HSD Test) [26] is also applied to test the significance of the differences between different methods' performance on stability and prediction accuracy.

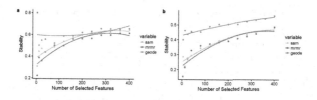

**Fig. 1.** Stability of feature selection methods on MeHg data. (a) Experiment on high-dose group versus control group. (b) Experiment on low-dose group versus control group.

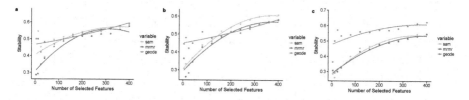

**Fig. 2.** Stability of feature selection methods on PCB 153 data. (a) Experiment on high-dose group versus control group. (b) Experiment on medium-dose group versus control group. (c) Experiment on low-dose group versus control group.

## 3   Results

### 3.1   Stability

We can see from Figs. 1 and 2 that the performance of GeoDE is more stable than SAM and mRMR across different numbers of selected features (with the smallest variance). Another big difference between GeoDE and the other two methods can be seen in low-dose condition of both MeHg and PCB 153: with all numbers of selected features, GeoDE consistently outperforms SAM and mRMR (Figs. 1b and 2c).

The results from Tukey HSD Test on stability are shown in Table 1. We limit the family error rate to 0.05, so the cases with an adjusted p-value (p-adj) smaller than 0.05 are regarded as significantly different. In accordance with the previous analysis, in low-dose condition both for MeHg and PCB 153, GeoDE is much more stable than the other two feature selection methods.

**Table 1.** Tukey HSD test on stability

| Toxicant | Dose condition | Comparison | p-adj |
|---|---|---|---|
| MeHg | low | GeoDE  is better than  SAM | 0.0006 |
| MeHg | low | GeoDE  is better than  mRMR | 0.0005 |
| PCB 153 | low | GeoDE  is better than  SAM | 0.0014 |
| PCB 153 | low | GeoDE  is better than  mRMR | 0.0007 |

**Table 2.** Tukey HSD test on prediction accuracy

| Toxicant | Dose condition | Classifier | Comparison | p-adj |
|---|---|---|---|---|
| MeHg | high | RIDGE | mRMR is better than GeoDE | 0.0107 |
| MeHg | high | RIDGE | mRMR is better than SAM | 0.0344 |
| MeHg | high | LASSO | mRMR is better than GeoDE | 0.0002 |
| MeHg | high | RIDGE | SAM is better than GeoDE | 0.0003 |
| MeHg | low | LASSO | GeoDE is better than SAM | 0.0004 |
| PCB 153 | high | LASSO | mRMR is better than GeoDE | 0.0003 |
| PCB 153 | high | LASSO | SAM is better than GeoDE | 0.0006 |
| PCB 153 | medium | SVM | mRMR is better than GeoDE | 0.0077 |
| PCB 153 | medium | LASSO | SAM is better than GeoDE | 0.0009 |
| PCB 153 | medium | LASSO | mRMR is better than GeoDE | 0.0009 |
| PCB 153 | low | RF | GeoDE is better than mRMR | 0.0002 |
| PCB 153 | low | RF | GeoDE is better than SAM | 0.0082 |
| PCB 153 | low | SVM | GeoDE is better than SAM | 0.0183 |

## 3.2 Accuracy

We find that the results of accuracy are not straightforward, since we will get different answers when asking which feature selection method performs the best. In each dose condition, all four classification methods are applied to assess the feature selection methods' ability to improve the prediction accuracy. Across different numbers of selected features, the AUCs of prediction are calculated. Figure 3 is an example in the condition of low-dose MeHg. It shows that SAM performs the best when the classifier is SVM, but GeoDE turns out to be the best with the other three classifiers. To make it simple, for every experiment (each dose of each toxicant), we select the best classification method for it: a classifier that can give a high prediction accuracy for all three feature selection methods. For example, in low-dose condition of MeHg (Fig. 3), RIDGE gets the highest prediction accuracy compared with the other three classifiers regardless of the used feature selection method. Then Fig. 4 gives us all results for all conditions. As we can see, different feature selection methods stand out as the best. In low-dose condition of MeHg and PCB 153 (Figs. 4b and e), GeoDE performs the best, because it has a higher AUC than the other two in most cases of different numbers of selected features. For the other conditions, in high-dose condition of both MeHg and PCB 153 (Figs. 4a and c), and medium-dose condition of PCB 153 (Fig. 4d), mRMR stands out, especially with a low number of selected features.

Another phenomenon we can see from Fig. 4 is that based on gene expression data and our analysis, MeHg appears to influence cods more than PCB 153 does, since it is easier for classifiers to distinguish between control group and treated group with a small number of features (higher prediction accuracy), and the performance is also more stable.

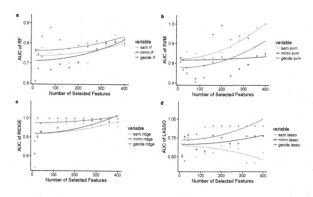

**Fig. 3.** Prediction accuracy on MeHg low dose data. (a) using RF (b) using SVM (c) using RIDGE (d) using LASSO.

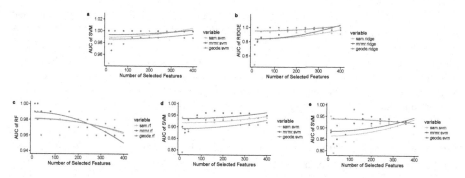

**Fig. 4.** Prediction accuracy. (a) in high-dose condition of MeHg (b) in low-dose condition of MeHg (c) in high-dose condition of PCB 153 (d) in medium-dose condition of PCB 153 (e) in low-dose condition of PCB 153.

According to the result of Tukey HSD Test on prediction accuracy (Table 2), in different dose conditions and with different classifiers, different feature selection methods will stand out. However, generally speaking, in high-dose condition, mRMR seems to outperform the other two feature selection methods, and in low-dose condition, GeoDE outperforms the other two.

## 4   Discussion and Conclusion

In this article, we have presented a framework to choose the most suitable biomarker discovery method for a specific dataset by comparing the potential candidates from two aspects: stability, reflecting whether the selected feature subset is robust to changes in the training data, and resulting prediction accuracy.

On the aspect of stability to find a reliable feature subset, our results show that GeoDE is more stable than SAM and mRMR in two ways: its stability varies little across different numbers of selected features for all conditions, and the absolute values of stability are always the highest for all numbers of selected features in low-dose condition.

On the aspect of feature selection methods' ability to improve a classifier's prediction accuracy, in different dose conditions, different feature selection methods show up as the best. mRMR performs well in high-dose condition, but in low-dose condition, GeoDE outperforms the other two.

To conclude this case study, the choice of the most suitable biomarker discovery method quite depends on the dataset under study. If the experiments are conducted in high dose, then mRMR is the best choice, since it gives the highest prediction accuracy and its stability is comparable with the other two. If it's in low dose, then GeoDE is definitely the best choice, considering its excellent performance both in stability and prediction accuracy.

The framework of the comparative analysis is not limited to only this case study, but can be applied to any other similar study.

**Acknowledgements.** We would like to thank the colleagues in Jonassen Group for helpful discussions and Computational Biology Unit at University of Bergen, where the work was carried out. We also would like to thank the Centre for Digital Life Norway (DLN) and the dCod 1.0 project to which the work is related.

**Funding.** The dCod 1.0 project is funded under the Digital Life Norway initiative of the BIOTEK 2021 program of the Research Council of Norway (project no. 248840).

# References

1. Ageeva, T.N., et al.: Gender-specific responses of mature Atlantic cod (Gadus morhua L.) to feed deprivation. Fish. Res. **188**, 95–99 (2017)
2. Goksøyr, A., Solberg, T.S., Serigstad, B.: Immunochemical detection of cytochrome P450IA1 induction in cod larvae and juveniles exposed to a water soluble fraction of North Sea crude oil. Mar. Pollut. Bull. **22**(3), 122–127 (1991)
3. Balk, L., et al.: Biomarkers in natural fish populations indicate adverse biological effects of offshore oil production. PLoS ONE **6**(5), e19735 (2011)
4. Sundt, et al.: WCM 2010, 2012. NIVA, IMR, IRIS report (2012)
5. Chesman, B.S., et al.: Hepatic metallothionein and total oxyradical scavenging capacity in Atlantic cod Gadus morhua caged in open sea contamination gradients. Aquat. Toxicol. **84**(3), 310–20 (2007)
6. Olsvik, P.A., et al.: Are Atlantic cod in store Lungegrdsvann, a seawater recipient in Bergen, affected by environmental contaminants? A qRT-PCR survey. J. Toxicol. Environ. Health Part A Curr. Issues **72**(3–4), 140–154 (2009)
7. Robotti, E., Manfredi, M., Marengo, E.: Biomarkers discovery through multivariate statistical methods: a review of recently developed methods and applications in proteomics. J. Proteomics Bioinform. **3**, 20 (2014)
8. De Winter, J.C.: Using the student's t-test with extremely small sample sizes. Pract. Assess. Res. Eval. **18**(10), 1–12 (2013)

9. Tusher, V.G., Tibshirani, R., Chu, G.: Significance analysis of microarrays applied to the ionizing radiation response. Proc. Nat. Acad. Sci. **98**(9), 5116–5121 (2001)

10. Yadetie, F., et al.: Global transcriptome analysis of Atlantic cod (Gadus morhua) liver after in vivo methylmercury exposure suggests effects on energy metabolism pathways. Aquat. Toxicol. **126**, 314–325 (2013)

11. Yadetie, F., et al.: Liver transcriptome analysis of Atlantic cod (Gadus morhua) exposed to PCB 153 indicates effects on cell cycle regulation and lipid metabolism. BMC Genom. **15**(1), 481 (2014)

12. Yadetie, F., et al.: Quantitative analyses of the hepatic proteome of methylmercury-exposed Atlantic cod (Gadus morhua) suggest oxidative stress-mediated effects on cellular energy metabolism. BMC Genom. **17**(1), 554 (2016)

13. Yadetie, F., et al.: Quantitative proteomics analysis reveals perturbation of lipid metabolic pathways in the liver of Atlantic cod (Gadus morhua) treated with PCB 153. Aquat. Toxicol. **185**, 19–28 (2017)

14. Shannon, P., et al.: Cytoscape: a software environment for integrated models of biomolecular interaction networks. Genome Res. **13**(11), 2498–2504 (2003)

15. Tong, A.H.Y., et al.: Global mapping of the yeast genetic interaction network. Science **303**(5659), 808–813 (2004)

16. He, Z., Yu, W.: Stable feature selection for biomarker discovery. Comput. Biol. Chem. **34**(4), 215–225 (2010)

17. Fawcett, T.: An introduction to ROC analysis. Pattern Recogn. Lett. **27**(8), 861–874 (2006)

18. Peng, H., Long, F., Ding, C.: Feature selection based on mutual information criteria of max-dependency, max-relevance, and min-redundancy. IEEE Trans. Pattern Anal. Mach. Intell. **27**(8), 1226–1238 (2005)

19. Clark, N.R., et al.: The characteristic direction: a geometrical approach to identify differentially expressed genes. BMC Bioinform. **15**(1), 79 (2014)

20. Nogueira, S., Sechidis, K., Brown, G.: On the stability of feature selection algorithms. J. Mach. Learn. Res. **18**, 1–54 (2018)

21. Davis, C.A., et al.: Reliable gene signatures for microarray classification: assessment of stability and performance. Bioinformatics **22**(19), 2356–2363 (2006)

22. Breiman, L.: Random forests. Mach. Learn. **45**(1), 5–32 (2001)

23. Cortes, C., Vapnik, V.: Support-vector networks. Mach. Learn. **20**(3), 273–297 (1995)

24. Friedman, J., Hastie, T., Tibshirani, R.: Regularization paths for generalized linear models via coordinate descent. J. Stat. Softw. **33**(1), 1 (2010)

25. Cawley, G.C., Talbot, N.L.: On over-fitting in model selection and subsequent selection bias in performance evaluation. J. Mach. Learn. Res. **11**, 2079–2107 (2010)

26. Yandell, B.: Practical Data Analysis for Designed Experiments. Routledge, Abingdon (2017)

# Short Papers

# Dual Active Sampling
# on Batch-Incremental Active Learning

Johan Phan[✉], Massimiliano Ruocco, and Francesco Scibilia

Norwegian University of Science and Technology, Trondheim, Norway
johap@stud.ntnu.no

**Abstract.** Recently, Convolutional Neural Networks (CNNs) have shown unprecedented success in the field of computer vision, especially on challenging image classification tasks by relying on a universal approach, i.e., training a deep model on a massive dataset of supervised examples. While unlabeled data are often an abundant resource, collecting a large set of labeled data, on the other hand, are very expensive, which often require considerable human efforts. One way to ease out this is to effectively select and label highly informative instances from a pool of unlabeled data (i.e., active learning). This paper proposed a new method of batch-mode active learning, Dual Active Sampling (DAS), which is based on a simple assumption, if two deep neural networks (DNNs) of the same structure and trained on the same dataset give significantly different output for a given sample, then that particular sample should be picked for additional training. While other state of the art methods in this field usually require intensive computational power or relying on a complicated structure, DAS is simpler to implement and, managed to get improved results on Cifar-10 with preferable computational time compared to the core-set method.

**Keywords:** Active Learning · Deep Learning · Image classification

## 1 Introduction

Over the last few years, Deep Convolutional Neural Networks (CNNs) have completely dominated the field of Image Recognition and proven itself to be a versatile and robust tool for achieving top performance on many tasks. However, as a data-driven method, it requires a considerable amount of labeled data in order to provide a good result. More importantly, the performance of CNNs, in most cases, better with more data, which led to a constant desire to collect more data, even though data labeling is a time consuming and expensive task. Aiming at improving the performance of an existing model by incrementally selecting and labeling the most suitable/informative unlabeled samples, Active Learning (AL) has been well studied over recent decades, and most of the early work can be found in [8]. With the rise in popularity of Deep Learning, especially in using CNNs to solve challenging image recognition problems [6], several attempts to develop an effective AL strategy on this field have been made, notably Coreset selection [7], where the active learner learn to pick the most representative

© Springer Nature Switzerland AG 2019
K. Bach and M. Ruocco (Eds.): NAIS 2019, CCIS 1056, pp. 127–132, 2019.
https://doi.org/10.1007/978-3-030-35664-4_12

data by treating the problem as a metric k-center. However, considering that the nature of DNNs are often complex and unpredictable, nearly all of the state of the art methods are often depended on the extracted output information from the networks as the selecting criteria, e.g., Wang et al. [10]. While this approach is proven to be effective, it has made the traditional serial AL, i.e., queries and re-train one at a time, less desirable. One of the main reasons is that DNNs are often slow to train and computationally expensive. For this reason, **batch-mode AL**, i.e., agent queries multiple samples at once, has become a much more suitable approach. As for batch-mode AL, one of the main challenges compared with the serial mode is the lack of constant feedback from the model for each selection, which often leads to overlapping of information between samples in a batch [8], i.e., the majority of them has similar features. Consequently, the goal of the strategies involving batch-mode AL is not to select the "best" sample but to pick the best combination of samples, i.e., the most informative dataset.

This paper proposed a new method of batch-mode AL, which is based on a simple assumption, if two DNNs of the same structure and trained on the same dataset give significantly different output for a given sample, then that particular sample should be picked for additional training. While other state of the art methods in this field normally require intensive computational power [7] or having a complicated structure [10], the method proposed in this paper is fast and simple to implement.

## 2   Related Work

When it comes to mapping the landscape of AL, the work "active learning literature survey" by [8] has to be mentioned. This paper has addressed all of the basic and advanced methods in AL up until 2010. However, the landscape of AL has changed a lot in the last few years. Followed by the rise of deep learning, most of the focus in AL has switched to supporting DNNs. Some of the notable recent works that put special focus in batch-mode AL for DNNs is, [10] and [5]. The former paper addressed the use of pseudo labeling, and the latter introduces a way to combine batch-mode AL with meta-learning.

In this work, core-set selection [7] was chosen as the baseline beside random sampling. This method uses an upper bound of the core-set loss, which is the gap between the training loss on the whole set and the core-set. By minimizing this upper bound, the authors show that the problem is equivalent to a K-center problem which can be solved by using a greedy approximation method or a mixed integer program (MIP) solver. Core-set selection is one of the current state of the art methods in the field of image classification for CNNs. However, both of them are very time consuming and could take several days to find the optimal solution, as for core-set selection is to solve an NP-Hard problem that grows exponentially with the size of the data set.

**Algorithm 1.** Dual Active Sampling(Simple)

Initialize *model*1 and *model*2 with pre-trained weight from Image-Net.
Initialize an empty Train set, S and unlabelled dataset, U
**for** *step* = 1 **to** *step* = N **do**
  **if** *step* < M **then**
    Query and Update S with n randomly selected samples from U
  **else**
    **for** i = 1 **to** n **do**
      random pick a batch of sample, **R** from U
      index = argmax(distance(model1(R),model2(R)))
      get label for R[index] and add to S
    **end for**
  **end if**
  **for** *epoch* = 1 **to** *epoch* = m **do**
    train(model1)
    train(model2)
    validate model1
  **end for**
**end for**

## 3    Theory and Method

In this paper, the proposed method is called **dual active sampling**, since it uses two DNNs with the same structure to perform the selection. **Dual Active Sampling (DAS)** or just dual sampling is motivated by the fact that a neural network trained on the same dataset tends to give slightly different results on different runs. In DAS, both DNNs uses the same structure and the same optimization parameters. However, due to data augmentation of the training data, using random image crop and random horizontal flip [9] combined with random dropout, after some training epoch, the internal weights of these networks can become significantly different from each other.

## 4    Experimental

### 4.1    Datasets and Experiment Settings

Because of time limitation, the experiment was only performed on Cifar-10 [4], which consists of 60000 $32 \times 32$ color images from 10 different classes. This dataset was then further divided into a training-set of 48000 images, a validation set of 2000 images and a test-set of 10000 images. In the experiment, only samples from the training-set got queried for labels. Additionally, the VGG-16 net had been chosen as the base model because of its simplicity, relative short training time, and powerful performance. The experiment was conducted on PyTorch, where the performance of DAS got compared with random selection and the core-set selection.

### 4.2  Implementation Details

The algorithm for the experiments can be found in Algorithm 1. The experiments were performed on CIFAR10 using VGG16 with ADAM optimizer [3]. The learning rate for both networks was chosen to be 0.0001, and only one of the networks got access to the validation-set and got tested on the test-set in order to save time. Both validation-set and test-set in the experiments were fully labeled. Additionally, the Euclidean distance was used to calculate the normalized distance between the output.

For every step, the agent added $n = 100$ of labeled data to the training set and trained its networks for $m = 10$ epochs. In the first two steps, the selection was performed randomly, while for the rest, the agent picked the sample that has the highest distance between networks from a pool of randomly selected samples. The selection was repeated for $N = 100$ times. This experiment was performed incremental, i.e., on each new step, the models got trained on the top of the previous step.

## 5  Result

In this section, the accuracy of DAS got compared with random sampling and core-set, both in terms of total accuracy and accuracy per class. The "full-set acc" in Fig. 1 is the accuracy of the model that trained on the whole training dataset.

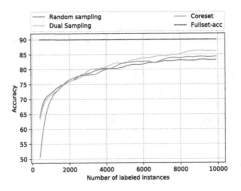

**Fig. 1.** Average test accuracy for Core-set, random sampling and DAS on 9 runs

## 6  Discussion

### 6.1  Comparison Between Dual Sampling and Coreset

In Fig. 1, DAS gave a preferable result compare with core-set selection in the beginning and surpassed the core-set method after it reached around 5000 instances. While most other AL methods except core-set tend to perform well in the beginning and get closer to random selection in the end, DAS seems to

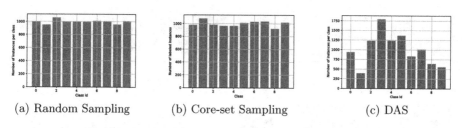

(a) Random Sampling         (b) Core-set Sampling              (c) DAS

**Fig. 2.** Distribution of items/class for 10000 samples.

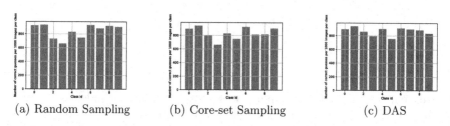

(a) Random Sampling         (b) Core-set Sampling              (c) DAS

**Fig. 3.** Correct classified item/class for 10000 samples (1000 samples on each class)

behave oppositely. Since DAS is depended on the output of the models, these models likely need to be stable and converge in order for DAS to work. In terms of computational time, DAS is both faster and highly parallelizable compare with core-set selection since the networks can get trained parallelly, i.e., if given enough computational power, DAS can theoretically be nearly as fast as random selection.

## 6.2   Distribution of Label and Accuracy per Class

In Fig. 2, the result of DAS shown a very unbalanced distribution of classes within the selected dataset, even though both random sampling and Core-set sampling followed the original balanced distribution of the Cifar-10. Besides that, DAS gave a substantial difference in number between class 1, 320 images of **ships**, and class 4, 1802 images of **cats**. By looking at Fig. 3a and b, in terms of accuracy, cats seem to be the most challenging class in Cifar-10 while images of ships seem to be much easier to classify. Furthermore, in Fig. 3c, while the model that used DAS selection had only be trained on around 300 of ship's images, it was able to achieve a comparable accuracy with the other results, which trained on nearly a thousand of pictures. It is also worth noting that in the case of DAS, the four classes in the middle got selected more often than the other classes, and they are also the classes that have the lowest accuracy in both core-set and random selection. By looking more closely at the pictures in Figs. 4 and 5, while the environment/background and object form are quite similar (sky and water) in the case of ship's pictures, the variation of background and form for cat's pictures is much more significant. This difference can explain why images of cats are more difficult for a model to learn to classify than images of ships.

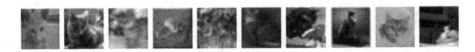

**Fig. 4.** Pictures of cats from Cifar-10

**Fig. 5.** Pictures of ships from Cifar-10

## 7   Conclusion

In this paper, dual active sampling was introduced as a simple yet effective method in active learning. However, the method still needs to be tested on more data set to confirm its effectiveness. The method was able to give an impressive result on the Cifar-10 dataset with superior accuracy and computational time compared to the core-set selection, which is found to be very interesting, provided the simplicity of its implementation. By looking at the distribution of selected items per class and the respective accuracy, DAS has shown an impressive behavior. It was able to select more samples from the challenging classes while maintaining a comparable accuracy on the less challenging classes, with much less sampling effort.

## References

1. Ducoffe, M., Precioso, F.: Adversarial active learning for deep networks: a margin based approach (2016)
2. Gal, Y., Ghahramani, Z.: Bayesian convolutional neural networks with Bernoulli approximate variational inference. In: NIPS (2015)
3. Kingma, D.P., Ba, J.: Adam: a method for stochastic optimization. In: International Conference on Learning Representations (2014)
4. Krizhevsky, A., Nair, V., Hinton, G.: CIFAR-10 (Canadian Institute for Advanced Research) (2013)
5. Ravi, S., Larochelle, H.: Meta-learning for batch mode active learning (2018)
6. Russakovsky, O., et al.: ImageNet large scale visual recognition challenge. Int. J. Comput. Vis. (IJCV) **115**(3), 211–252 (2015)
7. Sener, O., Savarese, S.: Active learning for convolutional neural networks: a core-set approach. In: ICLR 2018 (2018)
8. Settles, B.: Active Learning. Morgan and Claypool Publishers, San Rafael (2012)
9. Takahashi, R., Matsubara, T., Uehara, K.: Data augmentation using random image cropping and patching for deep CNNs (2018)
10. Wang, K., Zhang, D., Li, Y., Zhang, R., Lin, L.: Cost-effective active learning for deep image classification. IEEE Trans. Circuits Syst. Video Technol. **27**, 2591–2600 (2017)

# Ethics of Artificial Intelligence Demarcations

Anders Braarud Hanssen and Stefano Nichele[⊠]

AI Lab, Oslo Metropolitan University, Oslo, Norway
{anbh,stenic}@oslomet.no

**Abstract.** In this paper, we present a set of key demarcations, particularly important when discussing ethical and societal issues of current AI research and applications. Properly distinguishing issues and concerns related to Artificial General Intelligence and weak AI, between symbolic and connectionist AI, AI methods, data and applications are prerequisites for an informed debate. Such demarcations would not only facilitate much-needed discussions on ethics on current AI technologies and research. In addition, sufficiently establishing such demarcations would also enhance knowledge-sharing and support rigor in interdisciplinary research between technical and social sciences.

**Keywords:** Artificial Intelligence · Ethics · Narrow AI · Artificial General Intelligence · Bias

## 1 Introduction

The original goal of Artificial Intelligence (AI) research was to create an artificial (electronic) brain. This idea was explored in the seminal work by McCullock and Pitts [14], where they proposed a network of simplified abstract versions of biological neurons. The goal of creating a full artificial brain with the same degree of intelligence of a human brain is still an open challenge. From the idea of a brain capable of general (human) intelligence, the interest of the AI community quickly moved towards simplified (narrow) versions of artificial intelligence, to solve specific tasks.

The state-of-the-art in (narrow) AI was described by D. Waltz on the Scientific American back in 1982 [18] as *"Computer programs that not only play games but also process visual information, learn from experience and understand some natural language"*. In addition, he added that *"The most challenging task is simulating common sense"*. The current state-of-the-art in AI has not changed radically from Waltz's definition. Today the most compelling and less understood aspect is still the simulation of common sense, i.e., reasoning and cognition. The scaling of computational resources has allowed advances in playing computer games, computer vision, and natural language processing, pretty much with the same methods used in the '80s. While the initial AI inspiration was the human brain, in the meanwhile several methods to simulate intelligence without neural-based systems emerged, e.g., symbolic AI. Such methods had a certain degree

© Springer Nature Switzerland AG 2019
K. Bach and M. Ruocco (Eds.): NAIS 2019, CCIS 1056, pp. 133–142, 2019.
https://doi.org/10.1007/978-3-030-35664-4_13

of success thanks to the less need for computational resources. The recent availability of massive computational resources has allowed scaling of neural systems with results that surpassed non-neural systems in most application domains.

In December 2018, the European Commission's High-Level Expert Group on Artificial Intelligence has proposed the following updated definition of AI [7]:

*"Artificial Intelligence (AI) refers to systems designed by humans that, given a complex goal, act in the physical of digital world by perceiving their environment, interpreting the collected structured or unstructured data, reasoning on the knowledge derived from this data and deciding the best action(s) to take (according to pre-defined parameters) to achieve the given goal. AI systems can also be designed to learn and adapt their behaviour by analyzing how the environment is affected by their previous actions. As a scientific discipline, AI includes several approaches and techniques, such as machine learning (of which deep learning and reinforcement learning are specific examples), machine reasoning (which includes planning, scheduling, knowledge representation and reasoning, search, and optimization), and robotics (which includes control, perception, sensors and actuators, as well as the integration of all other techniques into cyber-physical systems)."*

The current understanding of AI ethics is rather vague, due to the broad definitions of AI used in the literature, and do not necessarily reflect the aspects and demarcations within the research community, the algorithms and methods, the computing substrates [11], and the target applications.

In the remainder of this paper, we will outline and discuss some important AI demarcations which have strong implications for the ethical aspects and possible reflections to address key issues in research on societal impacts such as Responsible Research and Innovation (RRI).

## 2   AI Demarcations

### 2.1   Weak AI vs AGI

The first and perhaps the most well known AI demarcation is the one between Weak AI (also known as Narrow AI, Applied AI) and Artificial General Intelligence (also called Strong AI or Full AI). While Weak AI aims at making a machine learn to solve a specific task, AGI targets machines that can learn and perform any intellectual task. This implies that AGI has the ability to "learn to learn", as well as the ability of problem-solving, reasoning, modelling and planning. G. Marcus and Y. LeCun, two prominent AI researchers, while disagreeing in many aspects of the future of AI, agree on a list of seven points [13]:

- AI is still in its infancy
- Machine learning is fundamentally necessary for reaching strong AI
- Deep learning is a powerful technique for machine learning
- Deep learning is not sufficient on its own for cognition
- Model-free/Reinforcement learning is not the answer, either
- AI systems still need better internal forward models
- Commonsense reasoning remains fundamentally unsolved

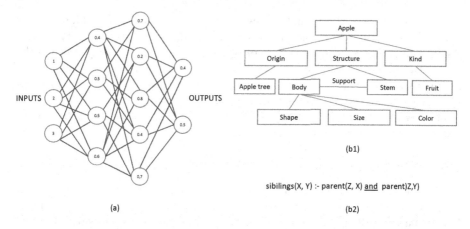

**Fig. 1.** (a) Connectionist representation where information is represented by synapses (red lines) between neurons (blue nodes). (b) two examples of symbolic representations, b1 with a tree representation and b2 with logic expression. (Color figure online)

It is evident that the demarcation between weak AI (all AI today and in the near future) and AGI implies that all current methods do not incorporate any form of commonsense reasoning, and the most used method of deep learning is not sufficient for a truly cognitive system. In addition, there is no current understanding or scientific theory on how commonsense reasoning could be achieved.

## 2.2  Symbolic AI vs Connectionist AI

Another important demarcation for AI systems is represented by the way information and relations are represented and encoded. In symbolic AI (also called algorithmic AI), knowledge is encoded in a symbolic form, together with rules to manipulate symbols and their relations. While symbol representation and manipulation makes it possible for a more rigorous study and explanation of weak AI systems, there is no evidence that the human brain is programmed as a symbolic machine. On the other hand, connectionist AI refers to a large network of units (neurons) that are interconnected together and encode/process information in a distributed way. While such models are more biologically plausible, they are typically data and compute hungry. Examples of symbolic and connectionist AI representations are depicted in Fig. 1.

## 2.3  AI Method vs Data

One demarcation that is often confused, especially in the context of AI bias, is the dataset used to train the AI model vs. the learning algorithm used to train the AI model (Note: the result of the training process using a specific dataset is an actual trained model, see next subsection). The fact that a trained model is biased is a feature of the AI model and not a bug. In fact, if one wants to model a real-world system, the actual real-world model may be biased. The training algorithm is transparent to bias and therefore should not be attributed for the AI system being biased. If the intention of the AI model is to be unbiased, then the used dataset (the sole source of bias) should be corrected. One example of training algorithm for neural networks is backpropagation. Backpropagation involves mathematical operations such as calculating the derivative of the squared error function with respect to the weights of the network. This type of mathematical operations does not allow for algorithmic bias.

## 2.4   AI Method vs Application

The actual trained AI model, and therefore the application in which the AI is used, is not to be confused with the AI algorithm or method used for training. This demarcation is very important as restrictions have to be considered at the application level rather than at the AI method and algorithmic level (i.e., the method may be the same in very different domains, and obviously with very different sets of data). An example: regulating databases. It is the wrong level of abstractions. What is regulated is the use cases of databases (e.g., credit card companies, or insurance companies). We regulate lawyers, not Word. We regulate financial companies, not Excel. We do not regulate steel companies, we regulate guns. And we do not ask steel companies to regulate guns. AI is not an application, it is a general set of building blocks.

## 2.5   AI vs Humans

Would regulators approve and consider ethically acceptable human-driven cars if they were invented today? Probably not. They are very dangerous by today's ethical standards. One important demarcation is human intelligence vs. artificial intelligence. Many of the issues with artificial intelligence are also present in human intelligence, e.g., black box. Can our intelligence be inspected when we drive a car? Is human intelligence open-source? Is the intelligence architecture known? Is the data used to train us for driving biased? Yes indeed. As we are given different datasets when we learn to drive. Is human intelligence deterministic? Can human intelligence be evaluated under different environmental conditions or noise? Are experiments repeatable? Those are all relevant questions to better understand the demarcation between human intelligence and AI.

## 2.6   Embodied AI

Features of the human cognition are shaped by aspects of the body (beyond the brain) [16]. Intelligence and cognition include high-level mental constructs (concepts and categories) and human performance on various cognitive tasks (reasoning/judgment), as a result of embodiment. Aspects of the body that shape cognition include the motor system, the perceptual systems, as well as the body interactions with the environment. It is therefore expected that artificial general intelligence requires embodied agents living in an environment. One may argue that weak AI lacks often embodiment and a reactive environment.

## 2.7  Compelling Questions

Through the description of the AI demarcations above, a list of relevant compelling questions for AI ethics emerged, and is listed below:

- What do we consider artificial intelligence?
- Are intelligent machines considered living machines?
- Can we demonstrate the emergence of intelligence and mind in an artificial living system?
- What ethical principles should be established for artificial general intelligence and weak artificial intelligence?
- What role do societal and ethical perspectives play in understanding the difference between human and machine intelligence?

# 3  Analysis

Based on the above synopsis of demarcations, we turn to how ethical and societal considerations are addressed within the generic field of AI. Current ethical and social science issues in and around artificial intelligence may benefit from a more rigorous articulation of demarcations within AI research. However, an overview of such issues would first benefit from situating applied ethics in new and emerging technologies.

Applied ethics as a discipline could be understood as relating to various practical applications of moral thought and principles and has a longstanding role within such fields as medicine, law and within various processions. In recent years, a range of approaches within ethics has addressed applications and implications of various ethical concerns within AI and machine learning [6,12]. Nevertheless, scholars have argued that merely addressing specific technical and ethical concerns in isolation may not be the most viable approach to the legitimacy of the future of AI research and applications [1]. The humanities and social sciences have gained validity when facing the many uncertainties related to societal impacts of new and emerging technologies. Arguably, AI research poses unprecedented societal and ethical questions both to the nature of such research and its outcomes. Thus, specific ethical questions and implications could also be seen in a broader context. Among such broader considerations are the importance of stakeholder involvement, transparency and accountability. Such issues engage considerations beyond the discipline of applied AI ethics and involve questions of governance and policy. As a consequence, AI research benefits from research addressing these concerns in particular. But what kinds of research incorporate these broader concerns and how does such research sufficiently incorporate the necessary rigor related to technical demarcations within various sub-fields of AI?

Within new and emerging technologies, ethical and societal considerations gained prominence after the surge in genomic research in the U.S through the Human Genome Project (HGP) under the label of ethical, legal and social implications (ELSI) [8] and later through its European counterpart ELSA. ELSI Research was seen as a necessary component of addressing potential social and ethical implications of the vast uncertainties related to genomic research, particularly through its commercialization. These avenues of research have in recent decades been applied to new and emerging technology areas such as nanotechnology [10], synthetic biology [3] and various ICT research [15]. After 2010 these research areas, through increased awareness of policy considerations combined through the term responsible research and innovation (RRI), which soon was adopted by the European Unions Framework Programmes. From both a research and policy perspective RRI emphasized the need to take the societal, ethical and environmental impacts of emerging science and technology into account. Simultaneously RRI has emphasized the need to align research and innovation with societal challenges. Nevertheless, research on applied ethics on AI and also RRI-informed research on AI is still in its infancy and is fraught with many shortcomings. Among these are establishing necessary demarcations and distinctions that are both epistemic and normative in nature. In fact, very few examples exist in current RRI-literature where a clarification between key concepts and issues in both research and applications are undertaken in a systematic manner. Such clarifications and demarcations would inform the trajectory of various discussions around ethics and societal impacts. Arguably they would also contribute to establishing a better understanding and learning outcomes between AI researchers, ethicists and social scientists. To further illustrate the importance of such demarcations in the context of RRI- or other forms of social science-based research, a few key examples will be presented in the following paragraphs.

Sufficiently distinguishing between weak AI and AGI underscores the need to separate broad debates on AGI from timely and necessary reflection on societal embedding of weak AI. Although compelling, AGI debates are marked by both dystopian and utopian narratives and based on probability and hype [2]. Moreover, obvious knowledge gaps in the current research frontier seem to under-emphasize the limitations of the current understanding of common sense reasoning and cognition in humans. Such limitations are currently making the realization of superintelligent AGI unforeseeable [19]. Nevertheless, the recurring worst-case scenarios and hype of AGI threaten the legitimacy of various weak AI applications and research in the general public. These debates may also overshadow the need to address pressing questions in relation to governance and regulation or areas where weak AI already is being implemented. Moreover, weak AI-based research frequently lacks the presence of integrated social science and ethical perspectives in their design. Such perspectives may contribute to a broader understanding of challenges within areas such as machine learning. Designed on the semblance of human learning, it draws from cultural and social structures and extrapolates from them. However, a better understanding of how algorithms build on such structures would also inform our understanding of what they cannot do, i.e such as present solutions for any scenario.

The nature of algorithmic design also shows that ethical and societal issues may be of very different natures with regard to current symbolic and connectionist AI and thus also provide very different ethical and societal scenarios. Symbolic AI may have vulnerabilities related to the quality of the design and/or hidden bias embedded into the algorithm itself, i.e bias related to relationships or symbols within symbolic language such as representing 'nurse' as 'female'. Although easily correctable it shows that ethical considerations such as gender equality point back to tacit linguistic biases and cannot be seen in isolation. At the same time, symbolic AI yields greater transparency towards such bias. Connectionist AI, as in deep neural networks, represents concerns more related to accountability and lack of transparency of what now seems to be 'black box-issues'. These may involve biases embedded in the data sets, such as societal, linguistic, cultural and heuristic biases that are embedded in data while at the same time present correlations that are context-sensitive, such as deep neural networks that may successfully predict sexual orientation by image analysis [20]. Further, by being 'data-hungry', connectionist AI seems vulnerable to error if data sets are not sufficiently substantial. Thus, in this regard ethical discourse around symbolic AI may yield results swiftly while in various connectionist AI context-of-use scenarios may be the most viable area of study.

The demarcation between the trained (applied) AI model and the training algorithm should inform what forms of ethical considerations are addressed; considerations that may often be misplaced. Some scholars argue regulation and law should primarily focus on the use of the model while the training algorithm itself could be considered as merely a tool [17]. Others argue that regulation and standardization are equally important in both [9]. Nevertheless, arguments that the training algorithms themselves are biased could be resolved by a proper demarcation between the training algorithm and application of the model. However, more research on the value-assumptions embedded in algorithmic training is needed, particularly in the discrepancy of the data embedded in the training algorithm and real-life scenarios [5]. Beyond these demarcations, there are different ethical considerations to be accounted for in the role that certain data sets play in the model and how an AI-tool is applied to various decision-making situations. In particular, if the bias is unknown or unidentified before the model is implemented it may have downstream impacts. Thus, in a range of scenarios, considerations such as distributive justice and or privacy may engage concerns related to both the training algorithm and the applied model. The data used in the training algorithm and the context of which the trained model is applied may in different ways combine to produce a complex set of urgent ethical and societal considerations. Nevertheless, distinguishing between the algorithm itself and the application of the model may itself resolve a range of unnecessary discussions about AI bias.

The distinction and/or similarities between human and artificial intelligence in relation to autonomous systems points to a discussion about the role of 'ethical algorithms' that in many situations may be a misplaced concern. Albeit debates of whether the 'Trolley-problem' poses a contrived and unrealistic dilemma between utilitarianist and deontological reasoning in real-life scenarios [4], its resolution may reside elsewhere. Both humans and autonomous systems opaque reasoning may in decision-making situations pose unreasonable risks and uncertainties. However, as of yet, the unforeseen consequences of outsourcing legal agency and responsibility from humans to autonomous systems may potentially be a more considerable societal risk. The incommensurability of legal, ethical and scientific reasoning may here be a more pressing subject than making algorithms 'ethical' and should address such issues as the problem of legal accountability. To what extent may we accept bias in humans while not in autonomous systems if we consider autonomous systems bias to be a liability? Some may argue that ethical considerations for humans and machines should be considered distinct and separate. Humans are by default prone to error while legally accountable. Machines, who we seek to error-correct all the time, may be equally imperfect while in particular scenarios present algorithmic decision-making that seems ethically 'superior' to human action. While the question remains if we should base moral judgments on the outcomes or intention of an action, demarcating human and machine 'ethics' is a pressing concern. It would at least seem important to define what moral status human and machine action have when they are equally nontransparent. However opaque, human intelligence is a product of adaptation to the environment. This embodied aspect of intelligence may at least provide us with a demarcation between machine and human intelligence (embodied vs disembodied). Weak AI, by virtue of lacking embodiment, substantially differs in nature from human intelligence. It would thus follow that there should be other ethical considerations (i.e moral rights and obligations) for weak AI systems than embodied systems.

## 4    Conclusions

For the purpose of our discussion, a substantial part of the current debate about AGI evolves around threats and promise based on speculation. However, such concerns are less pressing and bound by considerable uncertainties and unresolved scientific challenges to develop a fully cognitive system. We argue that a proper demarcation between AGI and weak AI would facilitate a more informed debate about pressing concerns related to challenges and opportunities. Such scenarios are worthy of discussion, not only for ethicists but for AI research institutions, policy-makers and for society-at-large. Further, when ethical and societal impacts are discussed, a distinction between issues related to connectionist and symbolic AI is needed to be able to identify both vulnerabilities, risks and countermeasures. Similarly, in discussing AI bias, distinguishing between the AI method and the bias embedded into the data, the training algorithm itself and the trained model would resolve uncertainties and identify how and to what extent bias should play a role in training algorithms. Further, it would clarify where ethical and societal issues may most adequately be identified. Sufficiently clarifying the difference between human and machine ethics points back to the insufficient demarcation between human and machine reasoning which is often equally opaque. Such a clarification would inform the debate on how to proceed with developing a more feasible 'machine ethics' and 'ethical algorithms', and potentially point the attention to issues of legal accountability.

It has been the overarching objective of this paper to illustrate the need for more rigor in the discourse on ethical and societal impacts of AI research in relation to a lack of sufficiently demarcating between key features of AI methods and tools. By providing illustrations of key demarcations, we have also suggested to what extent this may inform research on ethical and societal issues, both on weak AI and AGI. Further, through establishing the relevance such demarcations in the context of ethical and societal impacts, a range of ongoing discussions about AI could adopt them to provide a more nuanced and more elaborate dialogue across disciplinary boundaries. In particular, such a broader approach to ethical and societal impacts of AI should shift focus from isolated and narrow ethical questions to include governance and regulatory considerations and facilitate knowledge-sharing among stakeholders. However, approaches such as RRI may not successfully engage in knowledge-sharing with AI researchers if the aforementioned demarcations are not taken sufficiently into account.

# References

1. Cath, C.: Governing artificial intelligence: ethical, legal and technical opportunities and challenges (2018)
2. Cave, S., et al.: Portrayals and perceptions of AI and why they matter (2018)
3. Coenen, C., Hennen, L., Link, H.: The ethics of synthetic biology. Contours of an emerging discourse. Technikfolgenabschätzung–Theorie und Praxis 18(2), 82–87 (2009)
4. De Freitas, J., Anthony, S.E., Alvarez, G.: Doubting driverless dilemmas (2019)
5. Dent, K.: Ethical considerations for AI researchers. In: 2018 AAAI Spring Symposium Series (2018)
6. Etzioni, A., Etzioni, O.: Incorporating ethics into artificial intelligence. J. Ethics 21(4), 403–418 (2017)
7. EU: A definition of AI: main capabilities and scientific disciplines. High-level expert group on artificial intelligence - Reports and Studies (2018). https://ec.europa.eu/digital-single-market/en/news/definition-artificial-intelligence-main-capabilities-and-scientific-disciplines
8. Fisher, E.: Lessons learned from the ethical, legal and social implications program (ELSI): planning societal implications research for the national nanotechnology program. Technol. Soc. 27(3), 321–328 (2005)
9. Goodman, B., Flaxman, S.: European union regulations on algorithmic decision-making and a "right to explanation". AI Mag. 38(3), 50–57 (2017)
10. Hullmann, A.: European activities in the field of ethical, legal and social aspects (ELSA) and governance of nanotechnology. DG Research, European Commission, Brussels (2008)
11. Konkoli, Z., Stepney, S., Broersma, H., Dini, P., Nehaniv, C.L., Nichele, S.: Philosophy of computation. Computational Matter. NCS, pp. 153–184. Springer, Cham (2018). https://doi.org/10.1007/978-3-319-65826-1_10
12. Luxton, D.D.: Artificial Intelligence in Behavioral and Mental Health Care. Academic Press, Cambridge (2015)
13. Marcus, G., LeCun, Y.: Does AI need a more innate machinery? Debate between Yann LeCun and Gary Marcus at NYU, 5 October 2017. Moderated by David Chalmers. Debate sponsored by the NYU center for Mind, Brain, and Consciousness. https://www.youtube.com/watch?v=vdWPQ6iAkT4

14. McCulloch, W.S., Pitts, W.: A logical calculus of the ideas immanent in nervous activity. Bull. Math. Biophys. **5**(4), 115–133 (1943)
15. Nydal, R., Myhr, A.I., Myskja, B.K.: From ethics of restriction to ethics of construction: ELSA research in Norway. Nordic J. Sci. Technol. Stud. **3**(1), 34–45 (2015)
16. Pfeifer, R., Bongard, J.: How the Body Shapes the Way We Think: A New View of Intelligence. MIT Press, Cambridge (2006)
17. Vayena, E., Blasimme, A., Cohen, I.G.: Machine learning in medicine: addressing ethical challenges. PLoS Med. **15**(11), e1002689 (2018)
18. Waltz, D.L.: Artificial intelligence. Sci. Am. **247**(4), 118–135 (1982). http://www.jstor.org/stable/24966706
19. Wang, P., Liu, K., Dougherty, Q.: Conceptions of artificial intelligence and singularity. Information **9**(4), 79 (2018)
20. Wang, Y., Kosinski, M.: Deep neural networks are more accurate than humans at detecting sexual orientation from facial images. J. Pers. Soc. Psychol. **114**(2), 246 (2018)

# Similarity Measure Development for Case-Based Reasoning–A Data-Driven Approach

Deepika Verma[1]([✉]), Kerstin Bach[1]￼, and Paul Jarle Mork[2]￼

[1] Department of Computer Science,
Norwegian University of Science and Technology, Trondheim, Norway
deepika.verma@ntnu.no
[2] Department of Public Health and Nursing,
Norwegian University of Science and Technology, Trondheim, Norway
http://www.idi.ntnu.no, http://www.ntnu.no/ism

**Abstract.** In this paper, we demonstrate a data-driven methodology for modelling the local similarity measures of various attributes in a dataset. We analyse the spread in the numerical attributes and estimate their distribution using polynomial function to showcase an approach for deriving strong initial value ranges of numerical attributes and use a non-overlapping distribution for categorical attributes such that the entire similarity range [0,1] is utilized. We use an open source dataset for demonstrating modelling and development of the similarity measures and will present a case-based reasoning (CBR) system that can be used to search for the most relevant similar cases.

**Keywords:** Case-based reasoning · Local similarity modelling · Knowledge modelling

## 1 Introduction

CBR has gained popularity in the recent years due to its novel approach to abstract and transfer domain-specific expert knowledge into a user-friendly tool which offers appropriate reasoning for solutions to problems ranging from simple daily life tasks to complex tasks which otherwise necessitate expert guidance.

Modelling the local similarities of attributes while preparing a CBR model can be a challenging task for small and simple, and large and complex data sets alike. In this paper, we direct our attention towards the knowledge engineering process of creating a CBR model and present a data-driven approach for modelling local similarity measures using the openly available User Knowledge Modelling dataset[1] in the myCBR workbench [2, 6]. The main contribution of this paper is a methodology for modelling the local similarity measures using a data-driven approach. We will showcase how the knowledge stored in a data set can be leveraged to define strong initial value ranges for both numerical and categorical attributes and therewith moderate and stratify the knowledge modelling process.

---

[1] https://archive.ics.uci.edu/ml/datasets/User+Knowledge+Modeling.

K. Bach and M. Ruocco (Eds.): NAIS 2019, CCIS 1056, pp. 143–148, 2019.
https://doi.org/10.1007/978-3-030-35664-4_14

The remainder of this paper is organised into sections as follows: in Sect. 2, we discuss related work about the use of data-driven similarity measure development and its application in CBR, followed by Sect. 3 wherein we present our similarity modelling approach. Finally, Sect. 4 concludes the work presented in this paper.

## 2    Related Work

Similar to the preference-based similarity measure development framework presented by authors in [1,4], we are presenting a framework for modelling local similarity measures based on the data set available. Therewith we can tailor each similarity measure to the application domain. Using a data-driven approach for automatic similarity learning and feature weighting has been presented by Gabel and Godehardt [3] where they trained a neural network to induce local and global similarity measures [5]. While we are not automatically assigning the similarity measures, we use the existing cases to derive them.

## 3    Data-Driven Knowledge Modelling

In this section, we explain how we implement a CBR system that can be applied to find the most similar and relevant cases. We use the local-global-principle [5] for tailoring the similarity measure for each attribute and thereby build a knowledge model. Once the local similarity measures are defined, we continue to use weighted sum for defining the global similarity.

Some of the most common challenges for utilizing any dataset for developing a CBR system are the identification of suitable dataset context for the problem at hand, definition of initial similarity measures, representation of cases and determination of valuable cases for populating the case base. In this section, we first describe how we populate the case base and generate cases in the developed case representation. Then we present our method for utilizing a given dataset to model the local similarity measures for both numerical as well as categorical attributes.

### 3.1    Case Generation

Developing a case representation is the first step of the CBR system development. Depending on the domain and the available data this can be a challenging process on its own. For presenting our data-driven modelling technique, we use the User Knowledge Modelling dataset, which comprises of six attributes, five numerical and one categorical. The description of all the attributes is presented in Table 1.

The categorical attribute *USN* has four permitted values: *Very Low, Low, Middle, High*. Table 2 shows the data statistics of the numerical attributes in the dataset.

The case base is then populated by loading the dataset into the previously defined case representation in the myCBR workbench. A single case in myCBR is represented as shown in Fig. 1, where *User* is the name of the concept which comprises of six attributes present in the original dataset.

**Table 1.** Description of attributes in User Knowledge Modelling dataset

| Attribute | Description |
|---|---|
| STG | The degree of study time for goal object materials |
| SCG | The degree of repetition number of user for goal object materials |
| STR | The degree of study time of user for related objects with goal object |
| LPR | The exam performance of user for related objects with goal object |
| PEG | The exam performance of user for goal objects |
| UNS | The knowledge level of user |

**Table 2.** Data set statistics

|  | STG | SCG | STR | LPR | PEG |
|---|---|---|---|---|---|
| count | 403 | 403 | 403 | 403 | 403 |
| mean | 0.3531 | 0.3559 | 0.4576 | 0.4313 | 0.4563 |
| min | 0 | 0 | 0 | 0 | 0 |
| max | 0.99 | 0.90 | 0.95 | 0.99 | 0.99 |

**Instance**

| Instance information | |
|---|---|
| Name | User100 |
| **Attributes** | |
| UNS | Low |
| LPR | 0.48 |
| PEG | 0.26 |
| SCG | 0.28 |
| STG | 0.27 |
| STR | 0.18 |

**Fig. 1.** Case representation in myCBR

## 3.2 Data-Driven Similarity Measures Development

The local-global-principle requires both the local similarity measure on the attribute level and the global one on the conceptual to be defined.

Researchers in CBR domain face the challenge of balancing the input from the domain experts and the available data while modelling the local similarity measures for different attributes in myCBR. Having a criteria which can lead the knowledge modelling process is helpful for both parties. We therefore suggest to make use of the existing data in this process. While setting upper and lower limits for numerical attributes is straight-forward, assigning the similarity behaviour is not. Consecutively, we assume that local similarity measures for continuous numerical attributes are polynomial distance functions (due to their flexibility and better converging ability) and the question is how steep of a similarity decline should be chosen. Therefore, we focus on the polynomial function of the similarity measure for numerical attributes and our goal is to determine their degree. We use box plots for visualizing the distributions and variations in the data set and map this into modelling local similarity measures.

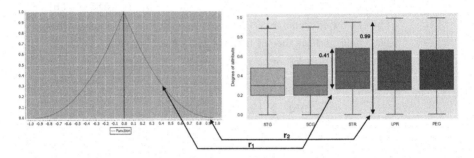

**Fig. 2.** Example for data-driven local similarity modelling: on the left there is a screen shot of a polynomial similarity function for a value range between 0 and 1. With the arrows we depict how the box-plot for attribute $STR$ relates to the decrease in similarity at a certain distance.

Figure 2 shows an example of a local similarity measure for a numerical attribute. From there we look into the $Q_1$ and $Q_3$, which indicate the majority spread of the attributes in the data set. In line with [1,7], we decided to take these values as reference points for determining the decrease in similarity.

Hence, creating a box-plot of the data set will allow modelling each attribute since we only take the Inter Quartile Range (IQR) and the range (min to max) into account:

$$r_1 = IQR$$
$$r_2 = range \tag{1}$$

It represents the difference between upper ($Q_3$) and lower ($Q_1$) quartiles in the box-plot, that is $IQR = Q_3 - Q_1$.

We assume that all similarity functions are polynomial and adjust the polynomial degree of the similarity function such that

$$y(r_1) \approx 0.30$$
$$y(r_2) \approx 0 \tag{2}$$

We can observe in Fig. 2 how the similarity function varies with respect to the attribute value after applying the methodology in Eqs. 1 and 2. The bigger the polynomial degree, the steeper the similarity function and more precise the attribute values in retrieved cases. The decline in the similarity function is steeper in the beginning until at $r_1$ it reaches close to $y(r_1)$ and then decreases gradually until at $r_2$ it is approximately close to $y(r_2)$. This way, the similarity function covers the entire attribute range as well as the similarity measure range $[0, 1]$. We use this as the initial definition of similarity measures.

While the local similarity measures for numerical attributes can be derived using their data distributions, assigning the similarity behaviour for categorical attributes can be challenging as it depends on whether or not there is a pre-existing relationship between the categorical values. In our dataset, the categorical attribute *UNS* has four permitted values which have an implicit relationship amongst each other. The local similarity measure for such an attribute can be modelled such that the relationship amongst the values is preserved while achieving the desired variation in the similarity measure in the range $[0,1]$, as shown in Fig. 3. In case of no relationship amongst the values, the similarity of one value to every different value can be set to zero.

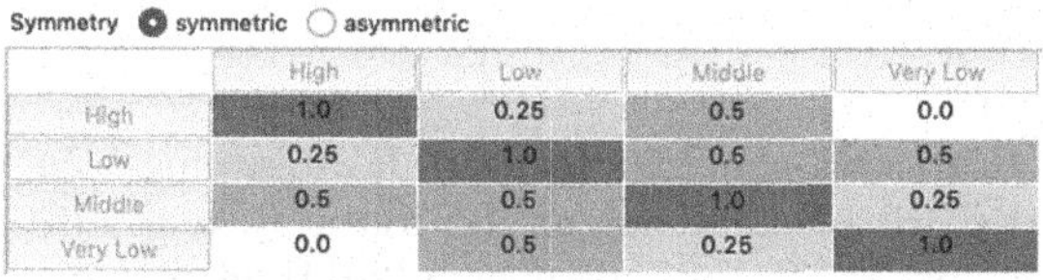

**Fig. 3.** Similarity measure modelling for non-overlapping categorical attribute

## 3.3 Retrieving Similar Cases

Once the casebase and similarity measures are in place, the model can be used to find similar cases. Figure 4 shows the result of one such query retrieval in myCBR. The retrieved cases are sorted by similarity value in descending order, that is, most similar case are displayed at the top while least similar are at the bottom. On the lower part of the figure, the four most similar *Users* are shown in a detailed view. The tool marks closer matches darker.

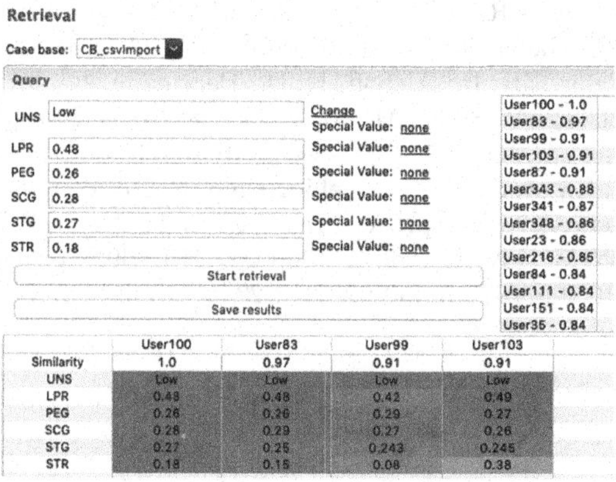

**Fig. 4.** A query and its retrieval result in the myCBR workbench

# 4  Discussion and Conclusion

In this paper, we have presented an approach to model the local similarity measures of a given dataset in myCBR in a data-driven manner. Our approach can be applied on any dataset to model the similarity measures. A more detailed evaluation of our approach can be found in [7] where we statistically evaluated its effectiveness using a public health domain dataset and showed that the CBR model created using our approach outperforms the k-NN regressor model in finding the most similar cases. The approach presented in this work can significantly reduce the efforts required to create new CBR models using different data sets from scratch. Therefore, it is safe to conclude that the approach works well on the used dataset and may also be applicable to other domains.

# References

1. Abdel-Aziz, A., Strickert, M., Hüllermeier, E.: Learning solution similarity in preference-based CBR. In: Lamontagne, L., Plaza, E. (eds.) ICCBR 2014. LNCS (LNAI), vol. 8765, pp. 17–31. Springer, Cham (2014). https://doi.org/10.1007/978-3-319-11209-1_3
2. Bach, K., Althoff, K.-D.: Developing case-based reasoning applications using myCBR 3. In: Agudo, B.D., Watson, I. (eds.) ICCBR 2012. LNCS (LNAI), vol. 7466, pp. 17–31. Springer, Heidelberg (2012). https://doi.org/10.1007/978-3-642-32986-9_4
3. Gabel, T., Godehardt, E.: Top-down induction of similarity measures using similarity clouds. In: Hüllermeier, E., Minor, M. (eds.) ICCBR 2015. LNCS (LNAI), vol. 9343, pp. 149–164. Springer, Cham (2015). https://doi.org/10.1007/978-3-319-24586-7_11
4. Hüllermeier, E., Schlegel, P.: Preference-based CBR: first steps toward a methodological framework. In: Ram, A., Wiratunga, N. (eds.) ICCBR 2011. LNCS (LNAI), vol. 6880, pp. 77–91. Springer, Heidelberg (2011). https://doi.org/10.1007/978-3-642-23291-6_8
5. Richter, M.M.: The knowledge contained in similarity measures. In: Veloso, M.M., Aamodt, A. (eds.) ICCBR-1995. LNCS, vol. 1010. Springer, Heidelberg (1995)
6. Stahl, A., Roth-Berghofer, T.R.: Rapid prototyping of CBR applications with the open source tool myCBR. In: Althoff, K.-D., Bergmann, R., Minor, M., Hanft, A. (eds.) ECCBR 2008. LNCS (LNAI), vol. 5239, pp. 615–629. Springer, Heidelberg (2008). https://doi.org/10.1007/978-3-540-85502-6_42
7. Verma, D., Bach, K., Mork, P.J.: Modelling similarity for comparing physical activity profiles - a data-driven approach. In: Cox, M.T., Funk, P., Begum, S. (eds.) ICCBR 2018. LNCS (LNAI), vol. 11156, pp. 415–430. Springer, Cham (2018). https://doi.org/10.1007/978-3-030-01081-2_28

# Author Index

Printed in the United States
By Bookmasters